Teaching a Child
to
Read and Write Well

Aunty Alice

PARTRIDGE

A Penguin Random House Company

To order additional copies of this book, contact
Toll Free 800 101 2657 (Singapore)
Toll Free 1 800 81 7340 (Malaysia)
orders.singapore@partridgepublishing.com

www.partridgepublishing.com/singapore

CONTENTS

PREFACE

This unique book is designed to guide teachers and students towards achieving excellence in literacy. It is the culmination of over thirty year's experience and research in this field, both as teacher and Principal. It covers all age groups and all needs, including slow learners, dyslexics, gifted children and students for whom English is a second language, (and all in between).

It has always been my concern that, in spite of a deluge of resources, teaching methods and innovations over the years, too many students still fail to acquire functional literacy. They stubbornly remain in the school system in spite of our best efforts to help them, and often emerge with low self-esteem and unfortunately, are often a huge cost to society. I searched exhaustively in an effort to discover what has been missed.

In the last ten years of my teaching, I was fortunate to be teaching in many multi-level classrooms that covered five to fourteen years of age. This required me to teach the children individually. While doing this, I explored, as part of my post-graduate studies, issues that focussed on children not achieving their potential. Thus I had in place the resources and context that would allow me to focus research and test teaching methods that examined the relationships between the literacy curriculum strands of reading, writing, listening, speaking, and presenting. It also allowed me to look more closely at the empowering or disempowering effects on people that are linked to language.

I used a student's written language as a place to start. Their efforts in writing, however humble, represented what their current understanding of literacy was, whether it is only a scribble, a picture, a story, a poem etc. It also laid it out for analysis for both student and teacher.

This initiated goal-based learning around their writing efforts and for many years I practiced this at all levels, and wherever I taught. I analysed thousands of pieces of student writing, collecting information as to what help was needed. It also became a very effective way to "listen" to children and engage them in their own evaluation of their efforts.

Out of these experiences, exciting discoveries emerged. My interest in the empowering effects of listening to the student in both oral and written language, uncovered much that had eluded me before.

One of my concerns was bullying, where one party loses their ability to speak or act. This is not the dictionary meaning for 'bully', but it should be. When I dug deeply into a bully's background, I discovered that the bully, focussed on silencing another's "voice" was trying to empower themselves, because they themselves had invariably been bullied by someone else; a neighbour, parent, sibling etc. I knew that[1][2] telling the bullied child to hit back or seek help did not work. But, giving the bully a chance to express all the hurt they themselves had endured and what it felt like, then working on their severely crushed self esteem, did. They almost invariably stopped.

Even more surprisingly, analysis of student writing revealed a structure of learning that is common to all students in acquiring literacy. It was not the structure imposed from outside by the present complicated curriculum, but an organic structure that was embedded in every student. It was embedded in Shakespeare, T.S. Elliot, Walt Whitman, and a million other outstanding giants in literacy. They had not been taught within a complicated structure but had been exposed to literature of quality, and a speaking environment of precise words that embodied thinking and communicating feelings. The structure was not in the writing content but was in mastering the symbols that allowed one to make sense of what they read and create meaning in what they wrote. I observed in my students that as they progressively mastered literacy symbols comprehension in their reading rose and so did their word knowledge, which allowed them to express themselves more confidently.

In my long teaching career I had not come across a usable and assessment-based structure that was easily tailored to the literacy needs of every student. Sure, there were many forms of literacy assessment that met the needs for accountability of schools and teachers and these were proliferating, (being propelled by governments who were increasingly alarmed at dropping literacy). This new way of looking at student achievement was the breakthrough I was looking for. It not only allowed me a door into the child's thinking, it gave me a place to set up true dialogue between us. It also revealed a clear path forward within this structure as to what the next appropriate learning step should be. This structure is well laid out in five stages of attainment in this book.

Analysing student writing attempts had paid huge dividends.

But I also researched what was known about listening and speaking. Going back as far as the foetus in the womb, I discovered that the sense of hearing is fully developed in the womb and the language centres of the brain are fully developed at birth, as they have always been. Also the brain is uniquely programmed for learning multiple languages up to about three to four years of age. Furthermore, most loving adults instinctively nurture language development by feeding in words and meaningful sounds. As one cannot think without words, the child without language finds learning difficult. Not just learning to speak, but to think about their own and other's experiences. This had also been confirmed by much research. Surely this was telling me something about the curriculum? Surely it needed to focus more on listening and speaking, as it was basic to all learning. But how does one do this without giving less time to the other strands of literacy?

The literacy themes identified in most school literacy curriculums are listening, speaking, reading, writing and presenting. They are poorly integrated and reading takes centre stage. Assessment methods and standards for identifying the reading age of a student and their place in relation to other children of similar age were freely available. But they gave little or no guidance as to a realistic place to start in doing something about their problems. The structure I worked with did.

Listening and speaking are not easy to teach. They are entwined with emotion, self-confidence, concentration, and prior knowledge. cultural background, access to words etc. (all difficult to assess and access). But if I thought of them as related to the other strands of the curriculum in a different way, it suddenly became clearer.

So I thought of reading as listening; listening to the author's voice by deciphering a code. And I thought of writing as speaking as an author, using the same code.

By analysing the student's writing attempts at expressing personal meanings, I could find a way into their heads to identify what their current mastery of literacy was. Using the structure I had discovered I could feed in what was needed, which in the early stages, was largely mastery of the code of symbols used to express oneself and understand what one was reading.

But as the code began to be mastered, one also needed to nurture quality in the message. This is, after all, the end goal that gives the student's writing its value. Both are inter-connected. If one is overly focussed on deciphering the code, often the message is missed. If one is only concerned with communicating the message, it may well miss its mark if it is indecipherable or the student does not have access to the words they need.

How does one develop quality in writing? It could only come from listening to (or reading) many models of writing, and understanding what words mean in context. This was borne out in the classroom where the best writers were invariably the best readers; but the reverse was not always true. Competent readers (those reading with 100% accuracy) were not necessarily good writers. This is where I focussed my research. What did I need to do to improve the quality of their writing, which with these children was often immature, simply constructed and lacking knowledge of the kind of words that were needed to really express themselves?

I discovered that hand in hand with lack of quality, even though the reading was accurate, it was not matched by comprehension. Many words they did not understand. This was mostly because the student had come from language-deprived environments, and had simply not been flooded with words by either having hundreds of books read to them or having very easy reading always accessible. The code seemed to become more difficult as they grew older because they had little understanding of how words were constructed, and did not understand words such as synonyms, antonyms, and common idiomatic expressions. All they did was confuse the picture. Also they did not have at their disposal words that described feelings that allowed them to empathise with the world around them. In other words they had not had enough words fed in, and their writing reflected this both in content and using the code.

Analysing their writing gave me a doorway into what I needed to focus on with these children. The most efficient way of getting words into their heads was to flood them with easy reading material defined as below their tested reading age level. They loved it. At last they had what they needed: opportunity to practice, opportunity to think, and access to words in context.

Hand in hand with this I offered learning that was built around children's interests as well as curriculum requirements. Particular attention was paid to words associated with science, social studies, history, economics, health, safety, sport, mathematics topics and the words associated with the instructional language of the teacher. Also listening to speakers invited into the classroom, taking part in discussions with others, watching films, doing computer research, observing and discussing artifacts etc. All were used to feed in language with which to think and then write. As children matured and had more and more words flooded in from their learning environment, their writing became more complex as it strove to demonstrate the nuances of meaning, feeling and organization of thinking that they needed to convey.

So analysing the student's writing was where I started in assessment. The student simply had to demonstrate in each piece of writing they did that they had achieved simple goals we had selected together.

Briefly, here is the process:

- Assess what students do in their writing to identify the stage of literacy they are at.
- Once having identified this, a reliable place to start in setting goals collaboratively with the student is established.
- Set up dialogue with the student as to what needs to be focussed on, what is achievable and how both teacher and student know when it has been achieved. Document this in a goal book so it can be focussed on at each student/teacher conference. This put the responsibility back on the student to become involved in the planning, and gives them their "voice".
- Feed in focussed activities from their reading (listening) to help them understand what they are aiming for.
- Assemble other appropriate resources for practice that embeds their learning in the long-term memory. (Refer to appendix and/or research activities that are available on the internet.).

Here is an example of this in action:

If a child does not put full stops in their writing, they are invariably not using them in their reading. Check this. They may be reading with one hundred percent accuracy, but their comprehension scores suggest there is a problem somewhere. Read their written work out loud, as they have written it (without full stops). At this point they often become frustrated at you reading their work in a funny way, not stopping until you reach the end, all out of breath. Discuss with them why you did this. Then go back to an easy piece of reading and have them read it to you. Often these children have come to believe, from their experience, that fast readers are good readers (adults) so they read fast, (being good decoders) only stopping at the end of the line as they learned to do with easy caption books in the beginning stages. Understanding was not the goal for them but fast reading was. You now have two goals:

1. *I will read easy books and only stop when I see a full stop, comma, exclamation mark and question mark. I am allowed to wait as long as I like.* (It gives time for them to digest what they have just read. The easy reading means they are not stopping to decode words)
2. *I will put stops in my own writing so people can read it better.*

Just using punctuation correctly, both in reading and writing, brings about a huge increase in reading comprehension for some students. Writing is much more readable and enjoyable for the target audience and a big hill has been climbed by the student in understanding their reading It takes not much more than two week's practice for this to be achieved. Time spent in dialogue with the child is saved in years of frustrating efforts that lead nowhere. Because of the common structure in learning literacy, there will be others in the room with the same problem. The teacher can therefore group children according to needs and they can monitor each other's reading and writing. Imagine what this does for their confidence! They now understand that reading fast is not important, but understanding the text by picking up the rhythms and flow of the author's thoughts is. Once punctuation with full stops has been mastered, the next thing is to indicate a new sentence is beginning so it must start with a capital. And so the structure unfolds, bit by bit, and this book helps teachers to focus on what may be appropriate next.

So no longer is spelling, reading, writing and presenting compartmentalized into separate curriculum areas, as has been done in the past. The whole literacy curriculum is integrated into only two strands, listening and speaking (aka reading, writing and presenting). Teachers and the curriculum must feed in what they want to get out. Reading (listening) is the channel through which examples of what has to be learned are presented. The student's writing (speaking) is the sample for assessment as to whether it has been achieved. The trick is to select goals appropriate to the level of readiness of each child and conference with the student regularly.

I sincerely hope the user of this book takes the trouble to read it carefully and initiate changes, however small, in their classroom management and teaching methods. The rapidly changing world is asking them to become collaborators and facilitators in learning and in this modern world many seek to abandon their traditional command and control roles. This book will open up a whole new practical approach to the teaching and learning process that will lead to success. It is what many teachers are struggling to find. It works right from the beginning and gets easier with practice. It will inspire teachers and schools as they witness change in negative attitudes of students towards their schooling. It promises confidence and inspiration for both teacher and learner and the process is extendable into other areas of learning.[3]

Because it carefully presents a structure in literacy acquisition, and is a well-trialled blueprint for success, it is ideally suited to parents who home school their children, and the school planning requirements at all levels from preschool onwards, (including gifted children at higher levels of elementary schools). It is also a useful resource for secondary teachers, all of whom are literacy teachers in a sense, but often do not know how to integrate it into their specialized subject area or where to start with non-reading students.[4] It is a guide for any teacher who truly wants to succeed with all children in teaching literacy.

But the true worth of this unique approach makes itself evident in interviews with parents that the student learns to lead in the company of their teacher. I was deeply moved at one teacher/parent/student conference when a ten year old initiated discussion with his father as to what he was doing and why, using his goal book and samples of his work to demonstrate achievement. The father's eyes filled with tears as he confessed this was the very first time his son had communicated honestly and proudly to him about what he was achieving at school. They both left hand-in-hand and a whole new basis for their relationship had opened up, based on trust, understanding and honest sharing. There were tears in my eyes too. That's what this book promises you.

Aunty Alice

WHAT ARE SOME BASIC PRINCIPLES THAT UNDERLIE INSTRUCTION IN LITERACY?

The goals of literacy instruction are to assist students to construct meaning from written text (reading) and to impart the skills necessary for writing with meaning

AT EARLY LEVELS

As soon as children make attempts to express themselves[5], support, acceptance, modelling and skilled guidance is essential to help them master an appropriate set of symbols to do this.

The teacher should allow the learner to choose what symbols to use, whether it be constructing a building with blocks as a two year old, drawing a picture, or writing words to go with their picture. If their writing skills are not up to doing it themselves, the teacher should offer to model writing for them by labelling their work, writing captions or writing stories to go with it.[6]

It is up to the teacher to assess readiness at each stage and to choose goals that are achievable. This book will help with this.

Basic decoding skills require dedicated instruction in the first two or three years of schooling but it is crucial that left to right progression and letter shapes and names be firmly established in the memory first. If children are having difficulty perceiving the difference in shape between *p/b/d/q,* or *u/n,* or *r /v,* they will not be able to recognize words/letters consistently and may well become confused or give up. As these skills become automatic, children's brains are able to focus more on word meanings in the reading context, and they begin to perceive patterns in words.

Simple sound patterns should be practiced for decoding visually (reading) in the early stages to facilitate this: For example, *cat, mat hat, sat, etc.* This is a necessary precursor to encoding (writing), as writing requires retrieval of words, phonemes and sound patterns from the long-term memory.

Ability to read new words rests on the ability to map letters and letter combinations to sounds and also understanding the context. For example, *can, car,* and *cane* are similar in appearance, so children need to understand how letters and sounds correspond to the context and apply this knowledge. For example, *I went for a ride in the car,* cannot make sense by substituting *can* or *cane* as it does not make sense in the context of *riding.* Yet all three words are very similar to look at. Children move developmentally from:

- Concrete letter-sound strategies such as: *This word starts with b and fits the context of the picture in the text ' Here is a ball'.*

- To sound-pattern strategies, such as: *I know 'cat', and this is the same, except it starts with a 'b' so the word may be bat,* (no picture support)
- To meaning-pattern strategies for decoding text. *I must have made a mistake with that word because it is talking about food here and "bat" is not a food. Perhaps it is 'banana'.*

Listening comes before speaking.[7] Reading is a form of listening, writing a form of speaking. Just as listening is where one began to learn to speak, reading and being read to is where one starts in order to write.

Writing involves several different aspects such as learning to write or form letters into words, whether by hand or computer; learning to spell; and learning to compose text. Success in writing is intrinsically bound up in reading and should be regarded as such in planning for success. In other words, go back to the reading to feed in what you want in writing.

AT ALL LEVELS

At all levels, high exposure to words ensures the various elements associated with a word enter the long-term memory for easier and faster retrieval. Prolific readers get this practice through their higher mileage, children with perceptual and language problems do not. It is important that there is plenty of easy reading around all children, including lists of words that have common elements. To only offer reading at their reading level for the child to choose from is a mistake. Children will reach higher reading levels naturally if a close watch is kept on their overall literacy development (accessed through their writing), and if they **are immersed in easy reading material and a literacy rich environment.** Easy reading frees up the brain to examine meaning, to examine the print more closely, to develop fluency and to ensure the reading is enjoyable and not tangled up in too many problems.

Reading and writing skills are most effectively taught concurrently and not in isolation. For example, through Shared Reading [8]children can learn how speech sounds connect to print and left to right progression. But additionally it will also help in many other ways such as developing their oral vocabulary, fluency, listening comprehension, prediction skills, and punctuation skills. Reading along with the teacher is a great model for all the various needs of the children in a classroom.

When basic writing skills have almost been mastered, much older students begin to think about language in creative new ways such as:

> *Is a poem appropriate here? Does it need illustration?*
> *I would love to tell this story as a film or as a cartoon*
> *I'd really love to paint this. How can I paint this view with words? A metaphor might best express what I want to say.*
> *I need a better word here but I can't think of one. Where's my thesaurus?*

If a student's thoughts are intended for public sharing, every effort should be made to ensure the message is clear. Drawing detail in pictures, and skills in the writing process are intrinsically bound up in this. It cannot be ignored and should be modelled and taught as well as caught.

However, everyone, (teacher, parent and student) should understand that perfection is not the primary goal. Effective communication of ideas without distraction is. Writers should not be restricted in their ability to communicate by their inability to spell or know the right word. They should be encouraged to write (or draw) whatever they know and their efforts applauded and analysed to detect an aspect that is appropriate to be introduced and mastered depending on the stage they are at.

One cannot think without words. Children who have not had words fed in lag behind others significantly in all areas of intellectual development. [9] It is important to read speak with and listen to children, allowing time to discuss new words, and to offer exciting, interesting learning environments. New words will not only assist thinking, it will assist thinking and encourage creative use of the imagination. This is where both home and school can have huge input. If intellectual and emotional growth is the goal, they simply need more and more words to think with and express their thoughts in order to clarify personal meanings.

Continued exposure to and study of words that explain people's feelings is very important. If they do not understand words such as *honesty, trust, tolerance, hostility, ambivalent, irrational, anxious, malevolent, listless, calm, serene, disinterested, etc* they will find it difficult to understand how the world operates. There are lists for reference in the appendix for all stages of literacy development. They are a great context for drama activities and group work. It is through understanding the meaning and use of these words that one is able to open up one's thinking to empathy with others. This will feed through into a better quality of writing. Importantly it is also what is needed more than ever in our games-console dominated lifestyles where there are no real consequences for one's actions.

WHAT ABOUT SPELLING?

Spelling should occupy a dedicated part of the curriculum only after the child has attained a reading age of seven. Up until then, every effort should be made to teach the various elements in words that make them readable.

Teachers need to know how spelling is acquired, how to identify what stage any learner is at, and how to facilitate progress to the next stage. Expectations for each learner or group of learners need to be realistically related to the stage learners are at. **These stages and resources to support learning at each stage are clearly indicated in this book.**

Ability to spell depends mostly on visual and auditory memory and the ability to perceive pattern. Perceiving patterns will lead to insightful risk-taking with regards independent word building skills. (Recognizing pattern in the environment and creating simple patterns should be part of the pre-reading learning environment as a precurser to learning to spell and master mathematics among other things).

Invented spelling should be encouraged as **mistakes should be regarded as opportunities for learning to take place,** and as such should be welcomed, not censured. Mistakes can lead to friendly dialogue between teacher and student, but to make mistakes, risk-taking is to be encouraged. The student's efforts, however small, should be celebrated first, then closely analysed in order to identify what is not known and not waste time on what is already [10]known.

Older students taking responsibility for correcting some of their own mistakes and learning new words is also to be applauded and rewarded. Computers can help with this at later stages.[11]However it is essential that all students be able to read the words in their spelling lists with ease before they are expected to learn to spell them. Small mistakes in a word indicate the child has almost mastered it. In order to attempt to read or write unknown words and also to see the sharp differences when words do not fit a pattern, learners should have seen a word or pattern often enough to know if words do not look right when they write[12]. We all do this.

It is helpful if students have ready access to word lists in the classroom because he/she needs to see sufficient examples of a certain element in order to recognize a pattern which can be applied again. Word pattern lists are in this book, broken down into levels. While the English language is mostly consistent and systematically patterned, there are, nevertheless, many exceptions, which eventually must be memorized. Research has established 3000 to 4000 high frequency words that may be considered basic for writing purposes. Unfortunately many of these do not follow a pattern or make sense phonetically (words such as *said, answer, their, do, they, who)*, but[13] students should always learn words specifically for their individual needs. That is why commercial spelling lists are not very efficient.

Successful spelling and reading both rely on the same mental image of a word. Therefore, **knowing the spelling of a word makes it more accessible for fluent reading.** But progress in reading will not necessarily result in spelling progress. Reading, (specially reading that is challenging), word study and the teaching of spelling through patterns is sometimes still not sufficient for some children to master spelling, specially children who do not read much or who have perceptual problems associated broadly with dyslexia. To put words into the long-term memory for easy retrieval, children need a personalized spelling list to learn. Words need to be revised at least three times to put them into the long-term memory before they move on. The words chosen to be learned should be ones they have almost got right in their writing, as well as some chosen from basic sight words. Spelling games can make spelling more fun, especially with these words. (Refer to appendix). The number of words to be learned by any one learner needs to be adjusted to their needs, abilities and motivation. Discuss with students to decide how many can be managed each week. This will empower them to make good decisions and take charge[14] As mentioned before, teacher expectations should be clear and related to the developmental stages of each child's learning. Use of this book will serve as in-service training for teachers and home schooling parents who may lack confidence and skills in this area.

Open communication between home and school should be maintained and homework taken for granted. Not all children are helped at home in spite of teachers requesting it, so teacher aide or peer support in this situation should be organized at school. Homework should only be revision of what has already been attended to at school.

IS HANDWRITING OBSOLETE?

Computers and texting have made handwriting seem not so necessary. But actual writing with an implement is still the easiest option in the early stages, as it reinforces memory for the shape of letters. It begins with the correct pencil grip and letter formation and progresses to connected handwriting with slope, (which enhance speed). Practice is needed and it is fun to marry handwriting with word study (such as the word patterns) and to do it to music or percussion. In the early stages learners should verbalize what they are doing in writing lessons and not be constrained by lines when they are concentrating only on shaping letters correctly. Also it is fun to use more than just pencils. Learning to shape the letters can be done in sand, with chalk, with fingers, pens, paint, collage etc. Once the shape is mastered, introduce lines, paper and pencils.

Good hand/eye co-ordination is needed for independent writing. If this is extremely difficult for some children, computers and keyboards could be used earlier. It is not always practical if there is not sufficient hardware for each child in the class and one must master typing skills to be proficient in using it. As technology advances these problems are rapidly being solved, but the teacher needs the expertise to put this technology in place and supervise its use.

But handwriting is a personal act that can give aesthetic satisfaction in much the same way that drawing and painting do. The receiver of a personalized hand-written letter often appreciates it and it connects the writer to the text in a more personalized way. Also, at later stages, learners get a lot of pleasure out of copying (in their best handwriting and/or different scripts) arresting metaphors, descriptions, alliterations, proverbs etc and illustrating them as part of art lessons. This is the time to introduce them to calligraphy and focus on fonts in the computer

Keyboard skills should be practiced by all students at some stage so students become more than one-fingered typists. It is perhaps better to rely entirely on keyboard writing at later stages than at earlier stages.

WHAT ABOUT WORK SHEETS AND GAMES?

I-pads and computers have a huge range of practice activities for students to use. They should not be done solely to amuse, but to learn and reinforce, so they should be focussed on individual need as identified by the teacher.

The teacher should assemble and have readily available needs-focussed individual or group work sheets, puzzles, word games etc, either in hard copy or easily accessed on computer sites in order to reinforce and revise spelling ability and extend understanding of the meanings of words. Students will then have practice activities related to their needs while waiting for conferencing with the teacher.

Activities for older children should aim to encourage thinking development by exposing the student to the meanings of words and word derivatives. They should be fun to do, perhaps with a partner, to encourage discussion and learning from each other. There is opportunity to access lots of word building and word meaning activities on the Internet, but again they should be carefully focussed on student needs.

PUNCTUATION

This is a crucial skill to master, first in reading, then in writing. **It should never be neglected** because in reading, understanding and using punctuation helps the reader hear the author's authentic voice. Detecting emotion and hearing the rhythm and flow of the words adds to the pleasure of reading and will aid enormously in understanding the text. I've seen student comprehension scores improve dramatically once they begin to master the reading of punctuation.

Using punctuation in their writing is an indicator they understand its usage to aid them in conveying meaning. Lack of it usually indicates they are not using it in their reading which is a serious issue. Use easy reading to master and practice this skill. If the reading is not easy they will be pausing to decode the text, which will defeat them.

Punctuation should be learned in a structured way, and never be neglected. (This book offers structured levels appropriate at each stage of development.)

DICTIONARIES and THESAURUS

These are one of the most poorly used resources, often introduced far too early when the child is unable to read them. **They should only be used if the student can read them easily, understand how they are structured, and are appropriate for the age group**; for example, aided by pictures at the lower levels.

A notebook can also be useful for a student in the very early levels of reading/writing, including word lists for reference that they can read but not necessarily spell. The child should be encouraged and applauded if they use other sources for words as well, such as wall charts, books, previous writing, high ability peer support etc. The teacher or teacher's aide can also be a "walking dictionary" when it is important that learners focus on the message/content only in their writing, and time is limited.

Dictionary and thesaurus usage can be taught by having children make their own "mini-dictionaries" on topics being studied. If they can demonstrate how a dictionary is constructed, even if only with a handful of words, they are well on their way to being able to use one.

At higher levels of ability, if writing is being done almost exclusively on the computer, spell checkers, computer dictionaries and thesaurus resources should be mastered and used to improve writing.

MEMORY AND FLUENCY

Memory and fluency are connected and both children and teachers should **understand how memory works** and how it is connected to fluency though practice.

There are two types of memory: working memory (which is short term) and long-term memory, (which means it can be retrieved much later, perhaps over a lifetime.) Working memory (short-term) is the gateway for learning but is easily forgotten.

Practice and revision are important if knowledge is to go from the working memory into the long-term memory for easy retrieval when needed. For example, slowness at recognizing words may indicate that previous words have faded from working memory before later words are recognized, affecting their ability to get meaning from the text. In this case the text is too hard. Hence there is the need for easy reading being always available to the student.

Decoding skills, words and word knowledge that are in the long-term memory lead to fluency in reading and writing. Fluency is the ability to read connected text accurately, quickly, and with expression. Fluent readers recognize words and comprehend at the same time. This is vital for students because they do not have to concentrate on "decoding" the individual words, which means they can focus their attention on the meaning. Fluent writing will emerge as spelling, punctuation etc are being mastered.

Repeated oral reading assisted by guidance from teachers, peers, or parents has significant and positive impact not only on fluency but also on word recognition and comprehension, so revisiting favourite books through shared reading is very important. Also having access to favourites is important even though the learner may be well past this level.

Choral reading can aid fluency and exercise the memory (e.g., reading aloud together as a group, or reciting text.) This can be great fun when various groups have different parts and different types of expression. Also different groups within a class can prepare text for sharing this way, adding drama and expression etc.

Tape-assisted reading, (for example, reading along with a recorded text), can aid memory and fluency.

Partner reading, (ie. a fluent partner providing a model of fluent reading), helps with word recognition, and provides feedback which can assist slower learners

Activities such as dramatizing a story make the re-reading task appealing and motivating. Students can rehearse and perform a play for peers. They might read from scripts derived from books that are rich in dialogue. Students play characters who speak lines, or a narrator who shares background information that are all great for fluency, memory and understanding the genre of play writing.

WHAT FORM OF ASSESSMENT FOR WRITING?

Government agencies are telling teachers that students are failing in writing on a vast scale. A range of tests made available to schools has identified this. Schools are expected to have their requirements in terms of writing assessment in their school well documented. The forms of assessment available are various and chosen in terms of what they will be used for.

Yet these assessment tools are still failing to bring about improvement. This is because many writing "tests" such as e-asTTle (NZ), have been primarily designed to produce summative benchmarks for horizontal and/or vertical moderation across and between schools to satisfy the demand for accountability. They are, in short, a rigorous, standardised assessment tool, and are used mostly for this purpose. They are an excellent resource, but time in a busy classroom is limited and the test would be difficult to do with every student more than once a term in its entirety, as it is too complex. It covers five forms of writing, has excellent prompts to inspire writers and has exemplars for the teacher to guide them in the marking of the test. In order for the e-asTTle application to calculate a scale score for a student, each element must be scored against a rubric. Students who score in the lowest category for every element assessed by e-asTTle writing are not well targeted by this assessment tool and they are the students who need the most support. For the day to day requirements of writing in the classroom, teachers require something simpler and which focuses on fewer issues. We are back to the curriculum being off target with the reality of teaching and learning for a lot of children, specially at the lower levels.

We all accept that writing is important. It gives students a voice to speak with that is more than speaking orally. Writing effectively and creatively allows one to communicate ideas and information and solve problems, and should, like any means of communication be a source of delight, comfort, amusement and learning. In pre-school settings and lower primary school settings one expresses oneself through the ongoing mastery and practice of symbol usage. These symbols may include models, dance, music, art, words, stories etc. At higher levels of primary and secondary schools writing becomes increasingly complex and there is much guidance for teachers and children who are quite adept at planning, peer-editing, drafting, self editing, re-drafting, crafting words and polishing one's efforts. As every writer knows this must be done if one is to publish it in its best form to the world.

But at any stage in the writing process the very act allows one to express one's thoughts for analysis by self and by others because it lays them out for the reader and the writer to make sense of them. The teacher and student can look at any piece of writing and discuss in partnership what needs to be mastered next to make it better for both parties. A simple goal should be recorded and the student held accountable to it in the next piece of writing they present. This should happen with any significant piece of writing, not just a forty minute sample done maybe twice a year over five different genre. For example, the lack of detail in a picture created by a five year old is telling you something. (They are probably not aware of detail and may be slow developers. So it is not much use introducing letters/ sounds/shapes that are quite an advanced form of detailed symbolism, until their pictures indicate they are aware of detail. They should be assisted by activities that encourage them to think about detail when creating a cake in dough, a building with blocks, or a drawing or painting. (Refer to Stage 0). Also a lot of time should be spent on picture discussion and teacher modelling. When they can create detail, they are 'reading' detail and are ready to use it in specific ways to express themselves.)

But for teaching, grouping, and accountability purposes, the teacher should collect regular, dated samples of the student's unassisted written language, whether it is just a picture or a written story. These ten-minute samples can demonstrate that progress is taking place. More importantly, students can discuss this progress in parent/teacher/student conferences themselves. (See later section on assessment).

For older children a ten-minute unassisted writing sample can also give a percentage of errors, an indication of what has been mastered up to this point and what has yet to be learned. It can also indicate the writing rate. If it is speeding up and they are writing more fluently in ten minutes, less time is being spent on figuring out the words, even though the content and mistakes may not seem to be obviously improving. The thinking skills and memory are becoming more automatic and words are being more easily retrieved from the long-term memory. It may be time to focus on other issues relevant to their stage of development.

RECOMMENDED CLASSROOM ASSESSMENT PROCEDURES

INDIVIDUAL WRITING SAMPLES

Twice a year take a formal individual writing sample. It should be dated, have the child's age clearly recorded, be on double line spacing, and should represent 10 minutes of unassisted writing in a genre form that suits the purposes of the teacher.

Before students start the timed sample, they should be given time to plan what will be written before they begin, so the ten minutes is spent writing steadily. For young learners the time should be halved.)

At the end of the ten minutes, give the learner 5 minutes (or longer) to improve their work and fix any mistakes and make notes about what each child does in this time.

USING WRITING SAMPLES FOR ASSESSMENT

Count and record the number of words written in ten minutes. This number can be compared with previous tests and if it is more, it suggests the learner is thinking faster and writing more confidently. If it is less, the learner should be shown the previous test and asked why the writing is slower this time. Discuss how they felt about the test: eg. were they anxious? Did they run out of time to finish it? did they run out of ideas before the time was up? The responses should help focus the learner's thinking. Then they should be asked to write a self-evaluation of their work and attach it to the sample.

The teacher should then analyse the writing carefully. It may show difficulty with some letter shapes, reversals, or transpositions of letters (which may indicate that the chid is having visual perception/ memory problems.) Underline the concern and put a number in the column beside it. A footnote-comment corresponding to it should be recorded. These comments help the teacher, not only with setting up ojectives for each child, but also to group learners with common needs.

Examine the kind of words being used. If the learner is relying only on words that they can spell, the sample will be strongly held together with basic sight words and may not have many spelling mistakes. This may indicate: that the learner is unwilling to take risks in trying words they can't spell because they do not have sufficient skills or knowledge in phonics, or they do not have a good feel for the genre required; or they have insufficient experience of a particular genre: For example, if it is a narrative, does the story demonstrate a sequence of ideas and have a clear structure? Is it original or a retell? How does it begin and end?

The teacher should then analyse the whole piece and make a statement of the child's most urgent needs according to their level of development and attach to the sample. Discuss this with the learner to select an area that can be focussed on (setting goals). Over time it will be easy to see forward progress or no progress. A copy of this analysis could also be in the teacher's records for reference in setting up class groups, and for assembling appropriate resources. It may also indicate overall class weaknesses that need further emphasis in the full class literacy programme: For example, teaching elements of a particular genre such as poetry, if one is expecting students to write it themselves. It is also very useful at parent teacher meetings.

GOAL BOOKS

Once you have writing samples you are ready to set up goal books for students. Allow space for them to record their own goals and evaluate their progress.

With younger children the teacher will need to model this, but encourage as much participation as possible by the student.

This goal book will be a resource to consult when there are parent/teacher/student interviews or when reports are written. As the year progresses, additional goals can be added, based on daily work efforts and can include other subject areas depending on how well the teacher can manage the task (bearing in mind the size of the class.) It can also include essential learning skills such as staying on task or having pencils and pens readily at hand. This will lead to changes in behaviour as the learner takes more and more control of the learning process based on their own evaluations.

The book needs to be available every time work is checked so it can be discussed with the learner, goals added, and comments recorded, by teacher, student and even parent.

For very early learners reward stickers can be added and the teacher will need to do the recording and reading of the goal book for the child. At this level keep it simple. You are training them in a method of managing learning. By the time they have used it for several years they are taking complete control of their own learning and the teacher has truly become the the facilitator.

A teacher can easily be daunted by this method when confronted by large classes of learners. I suggest the teacher begin with slow learners first, (which may only be a group of six to eight children, often with common needs).

As the teacher becomes quicker and more confident in this method it can be extended to learners with behavioural problems, or gifted children (who will quickly take control of it themselves). It won't be long before the whole class will be asking for this.

Time conferencing with each student means time not spent on class teaching and supervision of behaviour. Work sheets and revision activities can be part of their goals. They occupy learners while they are waiting for a conference.

A system of cards (or similar), that indicate when a learner needs to see the teacher needs to be set up.

10

The teacher needs to make sure they themselves have recorded these key conferencing times so they can check up on learners who are trying to avoid them.

Time needs to be spent on explaining essential skills. i.e., having gear ready and organized to begin work, not disturbing others, helping others, working quietly, organizing to fill time when finished.

REWARD SYSTEMS

Have a reward system in place for groups or individuals who make efforts to make the class a great place to be in. (This could be discussed at the beginning of the year as to what kind of classroom they want)

The following are ideas teachers may want to try:
Be the line leader for a week
Pick a game at sport/gym time
Sit with a friend for a week
Sit with the teacher and a friend for lunch in the classroom
Cook with a parent supervisor and three friends of your choosing.
Sit next to the teacher during story time
Teach the class a favorite game
Have lunch with the teacher and a friend in the classroom
Have the teacher make a positive phone call home
Send an e-mail home to parent re good things in your day
Enjoy a positive visit with the principal
Free time (say half an hour at the end of the week) with a friend or group of your choosing
Be the teacher's helper for the day
Choose a book for read aloud
Draw on the chalkboard or whiteboard
First choice of class job for the week
Choose music for the class to hear
Help in a classroom of younger children
Use the teacher's chair
Take home a class game for a night
Keep a favoutite stuffed animal at desk
Operate a film projector or other equipment
Be the leader of a class game

SAMPLE: GOAL SETTING

In the early stages teachers should model how to use a goal book. As the child becomes familiar with it , they can take more control in setting goals for themselves

Goal setting is very important for managing student learning. The following formats model a 'how to'. It can begin small in the very early stages (such as: I will learn to write my name), and as the student grows so should the use of it become embedded into all their schooling with more and more emphasis on students self-selecting their goals and evaluating their own work.

The tables below are not the only format but is one that has worked. It requires a double page spread.

Stage One Sample		
GOAL	DATE ACHIEVED	TEACHER, PARENT OR STUDENT COMMENT
I will read five words in my note book every night for homework	20 words: 12/6: (teacher sign) 20 words: 28/6: (teacher sign) 20 words: 16/7: (teacher sign)	I am getting better at reading my words I am proud of your efforts John (Dad)

I will learn the *b* sound and write the letter properly	13/6 (teacher sign)	You hardly ever get it wrong now John. Great! (teacher sign)
I will read ten words now every night for homework	50 words: 8/8: (teacher sign)	It is easy now because I can see the pattern in the words
Worksheets letter 'b'	(5) 17/7: (teacher sign)	

Stage Five Sample

GOAL	DATE ACHIEVED	TEACHER, PARENT OR STUDENT COMMENT
I will search in my reading for interesting ways that words have been used and record them	16/7: (teacher sign)	Margaret Mahy is very good at this Tracy. Will you share what you find with the class? (teacher sign)
I will try to use interesting words in my own writing	23/8: (teacher sign)	I enjoy using metaphor in my poems because it helps me write what I am feeling more clearly. (Sharon)
Worksheets descriptive words homonyms	(5) 13/8: (teacher sign) (7) 20/8: (teacher sign) (3) 27/8: (teacher sign)	
I will learn the class list of homonyms and show how to use them in sentences.		Come to me to be tested when you are ready (teacher sign)
Genre narratives√ book reviews poems story structures√ diary letter writing descriptions	14/7: (teacher sign) 23/7: (teacher sign)	Come and see me about how to structure stories (teacher sign) I like the way you showed me how to do book reviews. It helps me think properly. (Sharon)

CONFERENCES

Goal setting is an ideal opportunity for setting up regular conferencing. A record of dates conferencing takes place should be kept so that students get regular contact with the teacher. It is a written record of dialogue that takes progress forward.

ADVANTAGES
- Conferencing provides a sound basis for communication between teacher and student, teacher and parent, and student and parent.
- It is easy to do, easy to compare progress over time, and is contextual, i.e., it is related to a real learning situation.
- It is focussed on individual needs or group needs. It can be done on a daily basis for low achievers, used for group goals over a longer period of time or with gifted children who will quickly personalize their learning and take control. The more advanced students need less supervision, (say once a week), less advanced need more, (say once a day or more)
- It needs to be run hand in hand with a citizenship or essential skills for learning program. A reward strategy to encourage children to come on board needs to be set in place.
- Most students will gradually take more and more control for themselves, as they learn to keep focussed on their needs. They learn to record their goals and give thoughtful evaluations of progress on a regular basis. By the end of their elementary schooling they should be setting goals for themselves as normal part of learning.
- Written comments present lots of material for discussion at any time, but are particularly useful when meeting with parents. This reassures them that their child is getting regular attention to their particular needs, and understand better what is going on in the classroom. It allows the student to take the lead in sharing successes and problems.
- Responsibility for progress is thrown back onto the student.[15]
- It can be used in tandem with commercial type tests.

DISADVANTAGES
- It can be difficult to keep tabs on each child on a daily or even weekly basis in a large class.
- The teacher must change their own attitude from command-and-control to facilitator. This may take time and not a little courage. It should be started in a small way first and then extended as the teacher gains more confidence.
- It requires a change of attitude on the part of the student, which may take time, as it throws responsibility to listen carefully and discuss problems back onto them. They must understand that mistakes are opportunities to learn rather than evidence of failure.

- If beginning this new approach to teaching, it may be best to start with low achievers first, and in one subject area only, until the teacher becomes comfortable with it. Spelling is a good area to start as it extends naturally into written language and then reading. As the teacher gains confidence and begins to cement in routines, it can be extended to gifted learners and then into other curriculum areas and finally to all students. However all students often begin wanting it for themselves and may put pressure on the teacher before he/she has practiced the skills sufficiently to extend it.

- It can be difficult to conference each child (as it may take more than fifteen minutes) while keeping the rest on task. However with a citizenship programme in place where students are acknowledged for making the classroom a productive and pleasant place for all, it can work. Children also need to be trained to consult their goal books for ongoing tasks to be completed without coming to the teacher all the time. There should always be plenty of relevant practice worksheets for them to go on with.

- Each term the goals could be started again from scratch as it gives children a new start; also, the number of goals do not become unmanageable. As goals are achieved it should be indicated in the margin of the book (stickers?) so the teacher does not come back to them.

ASSESSMENT FOR PROGRESS ACROSS THE WHOLE SCHOOL

TWICE YEARLY WRITTEN LANGUAGE SAMPLES

Written language samples should filed by the teacher twice a year at least. Students should be encouraged to write their own comments about these samples. Samples of running records of reading, maths tests, art samples, science evaluations etc. (analysed in much the same way), can be included.

Also the school test, using an agreed upon type used right across the school, should be included and graphs made that indicate progress from class to class. This is the kind of information the Education Ministry require to keep schools accountable.

COMMERCIAL SPELLING TESTS

There are many commercial spelling tests/programmes available for teachers to use. They can indicate a level of spelling competency within that particular programme. They are often accompanied by a specific list of words related to the accompanying tests for the student to learn.

ADVANTAGES
- The student is getting some structured curriculum work in spelling
- The test results are useful for reporting to parents that the child is/is not making progress.
- The school has a consistent testing system across classes so can easily track progress from year to year.
- If the next class/school is using the same programme it is easy to ensure continuity

DISADVANTAGES
- It is often difficult to relate these tests to the day-to-day learning needs of the student because they are seldom diagnostic.
- If extended into the daily class programme, it can be difficult to keep tabs on each child on a daily or even weekly basis in a large class
- If students transfer to another school that is not using this particular programme the new teacher needs to begin again with their own school programme.

STAGES OF
LITERACY DEVELOPMENT

STAGE 0

Early attempts at writing (aged three and a half years)

READINESS

Children at this level are not ready to begin the formal reading/writing process, which necessarily involves spelling, reading and writing. But they can be identified by teacher observation of the symbols they do use to express themselves. They are usually ready to read and write when they can do most of the following:-

- Play imaginatively using toys and dress up clothes
- Beginning to draw simple pictures representing experiences
- Create models using blocks, dough, construction toys
- Solve simple puzzles
- Listen and respond to a simple story
- Observe and discuss detail in pictures
- Remember simple rhymes and finger plays
- Take an active part in talking with others

Reluctance to become involved in the above range of activities can indicate any one or a combination of the following factors:

- Reluctance to take risks; (There could be many reasons for this, such as parental expectations are too high and they lack the confidence to fulfil them; or they are shy or overwhelmed by the schooling experience; or they are worried about specific children who are too boisterous or have bullying tendencies.)
- They may have poor language skills because of hearing problems and/or speech problems; or they are from non-stimulating or non-standard English speaking environments
- They may not have the auditory and visual discrimination skills required to handle the complexities associated with letter shapes and sounds.
- They may lack concentration or have poor memory, and find it difficult to follow instructions or stay on task.

STAGE 0: TEACHER ACTION

Do not set up conferencing with the student at this age.

Schedule discussion with the parents backed up by the written observations of the teacher of the child's interactions in and out of the classroom and explain the stage the child is at.

If substantial delay in the child's development is suspected, arrange for a thorough medical examination to which the parent takes the teacher's written observations of the child in the classroom setting.

Provide ample opportunity to work in a pre-school type environment.

Assemble resources and structure environments that facilitate the development of the necessary skills in order to handle print. Specific activities that develop concentration, auditory and visual memory, finer listening skills, oral language, and finer motor coordination are to be found throughout all curriculum areas. (music and movement, physical education, maths, etc.). The trick is to have specific goals in mind. [16]

Create a learning programme based on specific skills they need, such as using word symbols. For example, create simple caption books related to interesting topics. e.g. "My Favourite Toys", "My Family" etc. The child can illustrate it themselves or cut our pictures or glue in appropriate photos. Use internet sites that teach simple language that relates words to pictures.[17]

Ensure lots and lots of stories are read to them, slowly, with opportunity to discuss pictures, and provide opportunity for lots of shared 'reading' and writing together.

The teacher/parent should model writing regularly (for example, an important piece of news, helping them make birthday cards, leaving notes for Daddy etc.) The parent and teacher should spell some words out as they're written and write very neatly.

Note: It is better that a child begin formal reading instruction at seven when they are ready, rather than experience two years of failure based on poor educational decisions at five. The progress compared to the average student may be slower to begin with but it will be there, and it will not be attended by fear of failure, poor behaviour, frustration, withdrawal, and ultimately social problems as evidenced by our prison populations who are often non-readers/writers.

Try decoding this:
✋♐ ⧫♒♓⬧ ⬥♏❒♏ ⧫♒♏ ♌♋⬧♓♍ ♋●◻♒♋♌♏⧫ ♋■♎ ⍓□◆ ⬥♏❒♏ ❒♏❑◆♓❒♏♎ ⧫□ ❍♋⬧⧫♏❒ ♓⧫ ♓■ □❒♎♏❒ ⧫□ ⬧◻♏●● ♋■♎ ⬥❒♓⧫♏ ⬥□◆●♎ ⍓□◆ ♐♓■♎ ♓⧫ ♏♋⬧⍓ ✍ ⬥♏ ♋❒♏ ♑♓❖♓■♑ ⧫♒♓⬧ ⧫♋⬧🙵 ⧫□ ♐♓❖♏ ⍓♏♋❒ □●♎⬧

❄❒♋■⬧●♋⧫♓□■ 📬📬📬 ✋♐ ⧫♒♏ ♋♌□❖♏ ⬥♏❒♏ ⧫♒♏ ♌♋⬧♓♍ ♋●◻♒♋♌♏⧫ ♋■♎ ⍓□◆ ⬥♏❒♏ ❒♏❑◆♓❒♏♎ ⧫□ ❍♋⬧⧫♏❒ ♓⧫ ♓■ □❒♎♏❒ ⧫□ ♍□❍❍◆■♓♍♋⧫♏ ⬥□◆●♎ ⍓□◆ ♐♓■♎ ♓⧫ ♏♋⬧⍓ ⧫□ ❒♏❍♏❍♌♏❒ ♋■♎ ⧫♒♏■ ◆⬧♏✍ ⬥♏ ♋❒♏ ♑♓❖♓■♑ ⧫♒♓⬧ ⧫♋⬧🙵 ⧫□ ❍□⬧⧫ ♐♓❖♏ ⍓♏♋❒ □●♎⬧📬

Translation:
"If the above were the basic alphabet and you were required to master it in order to read and write, would you find it easy to use?"

Many children on entering school have normal phonological skills in that they can hear speech sounds, but lack letter sound. It is well established that children who develop this readily do better at reading. That is the focus of the next stage.

STAGE ONE

Ability to draw detail shows readiness to deal with the details of print symbols.

READINESS

If children are noticing (reading) details in their environment and in pictures, they are begiing to show it in their drawings. They are now ready to deal with the detailed observation required to read and recognize letters and write them.

- The learner is securing alphabet knowledge such as using correct letter names, associating some letters to sounds and beginning to understand the difference between letters and words.
- There are increasing numbers of words that they can read on sight (out of context) as they experience more and more exposure to print. They are starting to remember the most commonly used words (their name, and words *like is, am, I, the, to, a, mum, dad etc.)*They are trying to write by making letter-like shapes.
- They are experiencing pattern in many areas of the curriculum. These skills of patterning will eventually flow into the literacy curriculum so they can construct knowledge for themselves.

STAGE ONE: TEACHER ACTION

A suitable graded reading programme is an important resource that most schools have in place. In its absence, you can create your own caption books, starting with one word captions, then two words etc., related to the child's experiences. The books may be created around colours, shapes, favourite toys, family, etc. Gradually introduce the sight words below.

At this stage the learner needs to recognize most of these words by sight alone: *I, am, come, is, can, like, here, the, a, come, to, and, Mum, Dad, big, little, my, this, we, went, on, look, at, said, going, in, on* plus any high interest words such as family names etc. that are used frequently in personal writing.[18]

The teacher can construct card games like Snap, Bingo and Fish to help establish basic words in the long-term memory. They should be put into personal word banks (cards) that can be referred to in writing. There are many fun resources on the internet for teaching basic words, letters and sounds.

The teacher should ensure high exposure to print through shared reading, games etc. Shared reading (using blown up books with enlarged text) should model reading, pointing out the need to wait at full stops, commas, question marks and exclamation marks so they learn to "read" the punctuation along with the words. First model it, then do it together, then do it on their own.

Letter knowledge is not simply reciting the alphabet. Learners need to be able to recognise and name all alphabet letters in both upper and lower case form. Computer keyboards are useful for teaching the difference between capitals and lower case. Have games that sort plastic letters or use magnetic ones to make words; have jig saw puzzles with letters etc. There are heaps of activities on the internet to do this.

In shared reading, ask children to tell you about letters. Ask them to give the name, the sound it represents, or a word beginning with that letter. Find the alternate form of it (capital or lower case). Look what happens if we put an *-s* on the end of this word! Can you find words that start with *-s*? What happens if I take the *-c* off *cat* ? etc

Don't overdo teaching letter sound relationships. At this level the student just has to be aware that spoken words are made up of sounds that are represented by symbols (called letters), and later that these sounds can be manipulated into diffeerent words.

The teacher should also model writing, (perhaps recording notable news items, the day of the week, the weather etc.) keeping it simple. The writing should be neat and accurate, as letters are easily confused. Occasionally spell out the words as you record them to reinforce the names of the letters. Also emphasize where the letters start, specially with easily confused letters such as *h* and *n*. Put these news items on newsprint, and, with the children, go back and identify common sight words and circle them with coloured pens. The children can cut them out and collect them for future reference.

They need to be able to shape all alphabet letters but may not have the size right. To do this they could trace over or copy under the words in the story that they have dictated to the teacher to help them form the shapes of the letters correctly. (First stage of spelling) This should be supervised closely so they start the letters in the correct place. Some children need to do this for a long time, until they are easily forming letters correctly and have firmly established left to right progression. Some teachers alternately put in place a printing programme. In my experience this not enough exposure and is often time-consuming to mark. Also it does not always ensure transfer across to practical contexts. However, a printing lesson to music where they practice writing letter shapes to the rhythm of the music verbalizing are doing with their hand is very beneficial. It gives high levels of practice and is fun. One needs to choose music with a strong suitable rhythm or use percussion instruments. Do not insist on having letters the right size. At the stage the correct shape is more important.

If there is a problem with holding a pencil correctly, give the student a short pencil with dots for the thumb and middle finger, on opposite sides of the pencil.

The letters should be taught in order of highest usage, but the student will be learning other letters incidentally such as the letters in their name.

The vowels are in every word and are essential for spelling, (but not so important for reading at this stage) so make them high priority, teach them early, and return to them often, as they affect the consonant sound as well. Vowels mainly have two sounds, usually referred to as the short and long sound. e.g. *e* as in *egg*, (short) and *e* as in *sea* (long). However, it is best to avoid referring to long and short sounds when teaching young children. Their concepts of long are often undeveloped at this stage and more likely to be thought of in terms of length of the actual letter, or in terms of size of the letter. This creates confusion for them. When the long sound is in the word refer to it as saying its own name. This usually happens when there is another silent vowel present or *y*.

The short vowel sounds need teaching first. They are difficult for some children to hear in the middle of words. Refer to a wall picture (such as *a* as in *apple*) instead. If they are curious about the long sound which is different, explain that *a,e,i,o,u* are letters that have more than one sound, They are special and can also say their own name. Don't expect children to remember this early on. It is better left till Stage 2. They are on a very high learning curve as it is.

apple (a), egg (e), in (i), orange (o), up (u) are key memory pegs for the short sounds of the vowels.

apple egg in orange up

Note: The Accelerated Alphabet Learning resource gives excellent guidance at this level. See end notes.

Children with hearing deficit related to constant ear infections, and children for whom English is a second language, often have trouble discriminating between the *e* and *i* vowel sounds. They need specific practice in listening carefully for the difference. Teach the finer listening skills necessary to do this by reciting aloud after the teacher, single syllable words with these sounds in them. (see word lists in the appendix). For example, *set, sit, fit let, lit, met mit, net, nit, bet, bit.* Students listen carefully and then write down the vowel they hear.

The consonants don't have a strong sound until teamed with a vowel. (If you teach the *b* sound as *buh* what about *be, ba, bu, bo, bi* ? Isolated consonant sounds are more a way of preparing the mouth to say them.

Sh, th, ch should be regarded as consonants because their sounds do not resemble the individual letters that make them. Here is a suggested sequence for teaching:

1. Learn the short sound of vowels
2. Learn all the consonants including *y* as *in yes.*
3. -*s* endings
4. *ch* as in *cheese*
5. *sh* as in *she*

6. *th* as in *the*

Later, when a child makes a spelling mistake, the teacher should study the mistake. If there is only a small mistake, for example, *se* for *she*, that's where you start. It indicates the child has almost mastered this particular sound. In this case the child needs work in discriminating the *sh* sound from the *s* sound. Give them a list of words to read (not spell) that are easy and includes the *sh*—sound: For example, *she, shed. shut, shoo, ship, shop.* If they write *het* for *hit*, they are not hearing the difference in the basic short vowel sounds *e* and *i* .

At this level (and when the child's work indicates they are ready for this), set up personal word lists in a notebook for them to practice reading words (not spelling them) for homework. The parent will need careful guidance on this as they sometimes think the child is expected to spell the words. Put a reminder in the front of the book for the parent or caregiver, or have a class meeting with the parents to explain your programme.

You will know when the learner is ready to begin reading word patterns when they are reading confidently on caption books at about Level 3 reading material (New Zealand) and remembering some sight words, (such *as is, am I can, said, to the, a*) The words need to relate to what is used in their writing or are learning in their reading so include sight words they recognize and include special interest words in their reading lists (their name, their pet's name, their favourite toy etc); ones that have arisen in their writing and which they can be invited to choose.

Over-learning is important at this stage as they easily forget. They need to revisit their reading word lists (which may be only five words or less to begin with) at least three times over three days for it to enter the long-term memory. Their notebook of reading words should be on hand when they write as they can refer to it if they want to use the words in their writing. Also the teacher can judiciously add to the list as new high interest words emerge in their writing.

Small simple word families can be included, (based on known sight words): e.g. *at, cat, bat, hat, sat,* or *in, bin, tin, sin, win, fin.* The child will gain confidence as this list grows and you will find their reading improves quickly as well. This is because they are getting high exposure to words, far more than is ordinarily available in the simple caption books they are reading. If they can read *am* in their reading book and they know a lot of letter sounds, it makes sense to give them *am, ham, Sam, dam, ram. jam, Pam, yam* in their reading word lists for practice of the pattern. (It has been calculated that a child needs to see a word about a thousand times before it enters the long-term memory and is effortlessly retrieved).

Although many teachers use them, a paged dictionary of teacher chosen words may not be a good idea yet as it is difficult for early readers to find a word they may want, if they cannot yet remember what it looks like. However many teachers use a dictionary card for each letter with space to put in high usage words under the correct beginning sound.

There are lots of activities and resources for schools to use to reinforce and give practice in letter/ sound relationships. One that is highly effective is *Accelerated Alphabet Learning* resource kit referred to elsewhere in this book. This resource covers maths, science, technology, music etc as integrated learning whilst learning the alphabet. It also facilitates multi-level group work in the classroom.

When writing on the board or for the child, the teacher should make every effort to be neat and tidy. Careless writing by teachers where letters are not properly joined, or do not touch the line, whilst easy for experienced readers, can cause confusion in early learners. Children sometimes confuse the letter shapes below. Use of the *Accelerated Alphabet Learning* resource will avoid these problems.

Teach the use of *an* instead of *a* when a word starting with a vowel that follows, eg. an egg, an old man

POTENTIAL PROBLEMS WITH THE ALPHABET LETTERS

p, b,q, d (all circle and stroke letters but they always cause confusion)
h, n (the first stroke of *h* is extended just a little to the *n*)
r, v (made the same way but *r* has no gap in the middle like a *v*)
m, n (m has an extra stroke)
t, f, (one is the other upside down)
u, n (one is the other upside down)
a, u (made the same way but the *a* is joined up at the top)
I, i, 1 (*one* and *I* are very similar)
e, c (made the same way, but start in different places)
g, y, j, i (can look similar, especially if the teacher is careless in their writing)
K, R (look very similar)
w, m (one is the other upside down)
These problems can be largely avoided if *Aunty Alice's Accelerated Alphabet Learning* is used as a first alphabet.

This is an example of invented spelling. It indicates the teacher should focus on the vowel sound *e* that is not known in *went*, and the *sh* sound in *fishing*. The learner knows two letters are needed for *sh*, and that one is an *h*, but is not sure of the other.

STAGE TWO

**At this stage the learner is writing letter symbols
for sounds they can hear in words**

READINESS

This is a very intensive learning time and the range of skills may be quite wide in the same class.

- They have a reading age less than seven.
- They are beginning to understand that the word *tomato* has an *m* in it the same as *mummy* and *coming* and can put down the beginning sounds of most words and even other sounds in words sometimes
- They can write all the letters starting them in the correct place.
- They can name some rhyming words and often enjoy nonsense words. *cat /mat / sat / fat / lat / jat.*
- They are beginning to write independently using a few basic high usage words and some sounds they hear. So they *ma rit like thes,* (which is invented spelling).
- Writing may be repetitive which may indicate they do not have sufficient skills or confidence to take risks.
- They are becoming more aware of patterns and word families and can read lists of words that have simple short vowel patterns. (e.g. *it, hit, fit, wit, lit*). They are beginning to accept that some words don't fit a pattern.

- They are reading words at their reading level, using context and some beginning sounds, but are not able to spell them.
- They are learning to use personal word lists, and go to other places such as wall charts, to search for words they need in their writing. Because they can remember where it is, and what it looks like, does not mean they can remember the separate sequential elements that go to make up the word.
- They know the names of the main punctuation marks but are not using them in their writing.

STAGE TWO: TEACHER ACTION

Often children at this stage think that fast readers are good readers. One must dispel this notion and ensure children are reading punctuation correctly as well as the words. This is a very important skill as it aids comprehension, allowing them time to think and hear the writer's voice as intended. Shared reading of big blown up books is a great way of modelling this.

Teacher should also model writing on big disposable charts or in their writing books, demonstrating how writing is done. As they write it is a good idea to spell out the words occasionally. Children can identify sentences by underlining them in coloured pens, (including the full stop). They can cut out or copy their favourite one, break it up and reassemble the words back into the sentence. They could copy and illustrate it into a class book of favourites. This also gives practice in starting sentences with a capital letter and finishing with a full stop.

Introduce simple contractions (see appendix for this stage)

Revise or teach as a reading skill, <u>not</u> a spelling skill:
- All the sounds in Stage One including the blended consonants such as st, br, tr, sp, st etc.
- sh, ch, th
- All the vowels as long and short sounds.
- The three sounds of *y* (see later)

Note: Formal spelling learning should be delayed until a reading age of seven is reached.

Reading family word lists, (not spelling), will train the brain to perceive patterns in words and give high exposure to vowel sound differences and consonant sounds. These patterns can also be reinforced in writing practice lessons, where not only the shape, but the size of letters now becomes the focus. Writing to music or a percussion beat is lots of fun, and a challenge if they have to get the size as well as the shape right. Specially lined paper can help.

The following sounds are contrary to much of what they have learned so far; that is, one letter is represented by one sound. They are now starting to be confronted with two letters representing one sound. Teachers should select a 'key word' to remember these sounds: For example, most children remember *car* so it is a good key word to help them remember the sound *ar*.

The following is a list to work on:

oo as in zoo
ee as in see
ou (house, our)
ow (cow)
ar, (car)
er (her)
ir (bird)
ur (murder)
or (for)
aw (saw)
ay (day)
all, ill, ell, oll, ull.
-ed endings *Note: -ed endings can sound like 't' as in jumped, 'd' as in played and 'ed' as in painted*
c as in *cut* (revision*)*
c as in *cell*
g as in *get* (revision)
g as in *George*
-ing (revision), *ang, ong, ung*
-ack, ick, eck, ock, uck
-ank, ank, unk, onk

Begin to show the effect of the silent letters: e.g.
- *e* on the end of a word: pip/pip*e*, Pet/Pet*e*, us/us*e*
- two vowels together (diagraphs): set/s*ea*t, men/m*ea*n, got/g*oa*t.

Note: Children can learn this pneumonic: "when two vowels go out walking, the first one does the talking and says its own name".

Silent *k* (know)
ight (as in *right*)
oi as in *oil*
oy as in *boy*
ph as in phone
wh as in where

y has three sounds, (and is one of the most difficult letters in the alphabet to master). It is a consonant when its sound is the same as in *yes*. It behaves as a vowel when it says *e's* name (as in *funny)*, and when it says *i's* name (as in *try)*. It can also act as a silent letter and indicate when a vowel is to say its own name. For example, *day*

Note: Avoid using the words hard and soft to describe the two sounds of g and c. Most children associate hard and soft with feeling something rather than hearing something. The soft sounds can be discussed at a later stage (c and g followed by e, i, and y becomes soft).

q is always followed by *u.*

Many of these sounds will be learned incidentally but some children require specific teaching. Monitor their 'invented' spelling in their writing to decide what you will focus on. Printing/writing lessons are a good place to introduce and revise these family words. You can see from the above list that this is an important stage to put a strong focus on sounds. It should not be expected that all children know all of these sounds before they enter stage three but it is important that they are being introduced to them. Do not expect them to be able to spell these words, merely that they learn to read/decode them. They will be revised when they come to actually learning to spell them at the next stage.

A child should not be expected to be able to spell a word until they can read it, and also understand its meaning. Children at Stage 3, when they have a reading age of seven plus years, could start on a formal spelling program. Fortunately, they will learn to spell many words incidentally on their own, e.g. their own name and words with high emotional attachment, and some sight words they have seen often. Celebrate this.

Focus on word meanings in their own reading and when reading to them. Students with restricted language development, non-standard English or English as a second language, may be unfamiliar with many words such as *delightful, chuckled, sighed, stern, wise, pleasant, enjoy, answer*

When reading to the class, tape yourself doing it and allow the children with non-standard English to take the tapes home along with the book.

When reading a story, the teacher needs to take the time to read slowly, pausing after turning the page to give opportunity for children to ask questions. Teachers need to express appreciation for the learner taking risks as often the question they may be afraid to ask is one that many need to know the answer to. Mistakes are to be appreciated as the child is then telling the teacher what s/he needs to learn. The child who will not take risks because they are afraid of being wrong is restricting their access to learning. This approach to teaching also requires a change of attitude on the part of some teachers.

STAGE THREE

**Children of this age enjoy working
with a partner and love to help each other**

READINESS

Children at this stage enjoy non-fiction books which give them information about all kinds of things such as the natural world, It is a wonderful opportunity for the teacher to stimulate this curiosity by making available a wide variety of easy reading material on these kinds of topics. Writing about them naturally follows.

- After a lot of practice reading patterns, rhymes, shared stories and graded reading materials, the student has now been exposed to hundreds of words and are fluent readers at about seven to eight years reading age.
- They are reading from sight (instant recognition of words at their reading level), most of the time and beginning to decode words of simple multiple syllables such as *looking, coming, mother.*
- They can write fluently and confidently with invented spelling that is getting closer to the correct form.
- They can perceive patterns in words and readily recognize words that do not follow expected patterns.

- They are more curious about words and enjoy simple crosswords, word-finds etc. They are very happy to take home work sheets for practice of skills. They love exploring word games etc. on the internet.
- They are using full stops, commas, exclamation marks in their reading, (mostly correctly), and may be using full stops in their writing.
- They are comfortable using a computer for their writing, and often want to join up the letters in their handwriting.

STAGE THREE: TEACHER ACTION

It is at this stage that word study and language work should intensify to widen their range of vocabulary. (Stage 3-5 in the appendix)

They need to understand that there are words (homonyms) that sound the same but are spelt differently *(e.g. their/there/they're)* and have different meanings. (see apendix) They need to be discussed and class team games set up to reinforce their meanings.

Also discuss words that are spelt the same but have different meanings. e.g. *wind (air blowing)* and *wind (twist); tear (crying) and tear (rip).* Students can create books to illustrate these words.

Students should now have the confidence and skills to be able to spell longer words. The teacher should extend syllabification skills training from reading multi-syllable words that they did in the previous stage, to spelling them: Teacher should model first, then student practice breaking words into syllables, (clapping first, then writing it in its bits).

The teacher should introduce new vowel diagraphs from the appendix and give practice using internet games etc.

They need to study gender specific words and plurals. (see appendix)

Actively teach vocabulary, particular 'feeling" words. (see appendix). A wide vocabularly will help the child in all subjects, helps them to think better and understand more.

At the next stage they need to be able to use a dictionary and thesaurus. These skills often need to be taught, as they are not easily caught. A very good way is for the teacher to have children construct their own "mini" dictionaries (lists of specific words with their meanings and perhaps an illustration, related to topics that are being studied). Knowing hpw dictionaries work makes it easier to use one. Computers offer spell-check, dictionary and thesaurus but they need training in using it.

They should be seeking to make their written work easily readable with neater writing and as few distractions in the form of spelling mistakes as possible. Teach students how to proof read and where to go to find and correct some (not all) of their mistakes. Help students to set achievable goals, e.g. *I will look up one word I know I have spelled incorrectly.* At a later stage, as skills develop and are practiced, the number of words they correct can be increased by the student as a goal. Teachers should have available simplified dictionaries or other sources for them to look up an increasing number of words that they recognize as possible mistakes.

One can reasonably expect that full stops, question marks, exclamation marks and commas are appearing regularly in their writing as a way of indicating how it should be read. The student should proof read their work and perhaps collaborate with a partner to ensure others are able to read their writing easily.

Writing lessons should expect correct shape, and sizing. Introduce slope into their writing lessons. It will assist speed, as will writing to musical rhythms, (which is a lot of fun).

Using quotation marks for direct speech could be started with some children.

Paragraphing skills should be discussed when teachers are modelling reading/writing to the class. Discuss why paragraphs are used. Go back into their own reading to study this too.

Formal individualized spelling lists to be learned should be started. The student can help construct these lists, and the words chosen related to mistakes they make in their writing. Unfortunately teachers often make the mistake of giving children words to learn to spell for homework which they can't yet read easily, or do not understand the meaning of.

Teachers should require students to be tested on each word in their spelling list at least three times so it enters the long-term memory. However, to test each child in a class of say twenty-five children at least three times is an unrealistic expectation for the teacher. Therefore home, teacher aide or peer assistance should be enlisted. The parent should be shown how the spelling programme works and should fully understand homework expectations.

Teachers should continually revise all previous learning and re-learn where mistakes indicate uncertainty. Work sheets and games that are appropriate to the practice they need, should be freely available. If they are easy, children enjoy taking them home for homework, and also enjoy working on them with a friend. Work sheets could focus on:-
-singular and plurals
-gender specific words, such as author/authoress, count/countess
-new sounds such as -*ew* (new) *and -le* endings (sparkle)
-syllabification skills
-locating and studying easier prefixes
-contractions
-double consonants
(see appendix)

Teach the following spelling rule: For words that end in *e*, *l*eave the *e* off before adding *ing*, for example, *come/coming dance/dancing* (Exceptions: words such as *see, be, tie*)

All the above are good writing lesson material too, depending on the age and ability of the child.

Teacher and parents need to continue reading to and with them a lot. They could begin to talk about the author's and illustrator's style. It can have great spin-offs into the class art program.

Encourage students to read extensively on their own (e.g., outside of school or during independent work time)

They should also be offered an exciting curriculum that includes a procession of new words entering the child's consciousness. New maths words should be available on a chart as they are often subject-specific and are easily forgotten (such as *quadrilateral, addend, equation*)

Keep encouraging them to ask questions when they do not understand. Celebrate this attitude to their learning. Also continue to celebrate their willingness to take risks.

STAGE FOUR

Learners at this stage are right into reading for enjoyment, excitement and knowlege and love chapter books

READINESS

School is a safe, fun place to be with their friends. A hands-on, active curriculum in a wide variety of subjects is of great importance.

- This is a very expansive stage and within this level there will be scope to expand knowledge hugely or to take it more slowly. Students could conceivably stay at this stage for two years or more, or until the end of their elementary years.
- They are beginning to master the more difficult sounds in spelling words and can read fluently.
- They are beginning to understand some of the idiosyncrasies of the English language such as irregular plurals
- They are extending their vocabulary through reading, hobbies, and a varied curriculum.
- They have been introduced to a thesaurus, and how its use can lead to precision in writing.
- They are beginning to take personal responsibility for spelling improvement and extension, and developing the habit of reading for pleasure. They love non-fiction books as well as story series.
- They are becoming used to homework assignments, which give practice of new knowledge.

STAGE FOUR: TEACHER ACTION

Encourage the learner to take personal responsibility for getting their spelling as accurate as possible. They should be proof reading and using spell checkers and dictionaries on computers to improve their work.

Teach how to do book reviews and have a programme of author and illustrator study. (The latter can lead to some interesting art lessons).

Have appropriate dictionaries and thesaurus readily available for each student at this level. They have already been introduced to a thesaurus, but now need to use it for more precision in their writing.

Teach the following tricky sounds:
-ie as in thief
-ould as in should
-ought as in bought
-alk as in talk
-ai as in air
-ign as in sign
-aught as in naughty

See the appendix for a list of troublesome words and have team games to encourage students to learn them.

Easier homonyms need to be introduced and studied. For example, *sale/sail, tale/tail, there/their/they're, bean/been, ate/eight* (see appendix)

Idiomatic expressions such *as ants in your pants, hold your tongue, hold your horses etc.* can be discussed. There are thousands of these in the English language and they can be problematic for non-native English learners. One can find what they mean on the internet or in an idiomatic dictionary. They can be fun to illustrate.

Homonyms, synonyms,[19] homophones, gender words, contractions, and 'feeling' words should be extended. Students should construct sentences to show they understand their meanings (see appendix).

Students should also study:
-prefixes and suffixes and their meanings
-opposites created by prefixes and suffixes
-root words in large words
-adding prefixes and suffixes to root words and how they effect meaning
-plurals of common troublesome words such as wife, tax, foot valley mouse.

Crossword puzzles provide purposeful dictionary activities

Work sheets for revision of the previous stage should be freely available.

Teach students how to generate and organize ideas before writing. The teacher should go through the process with the class or group, and then allow them to practice. Collaboration with a partner or a group is fun here, sharing the product of their endeavours with the class. It need not necessarily be taken to the point of actually writing it.

Instruction should allow students to adjust their writing through the use of different voices (e.g. write a letter as a fictional character, historical figure, or self). Students can also write for a variety of audiences and for a number of different purposes.

Study how to combine simple sentences to make writing more interesting and fluent. e.g. *Oysters taste good.* combined with *Dad likes to eat oysters.* creates a better sentence *Dad likes to eat oysters because they taste good.* This kind of activity helps writers with sentence structure and grammar.

Study how inserting descriptive words into otherwise plain sentences adds interest and paints a better picture for the reader. e.g. *The bumblebee visited every flower* could be written: *The fat bumblebee visited every flower often.* or: *Every few seconds the huge, hairy bumblebee dipped into every flower.*

Continue work on understanding text conventions such as paragraph structure. Ask students to take a text and break it down to its skeletal outline by identifying topic sentences. This helps understanding of how writers develop a story.

STAGE FIVE

READINESS

Students at this stage are becoming more serious about life and beginning to specialize in areas of excellence such as sport or gymnastics, writing stories, art , etc. The teacher needs to be a specialist in everything and, if not, enlist outside help to come in to inspire them.

- At this level students are now competent readers and writers and are relatively high achievers
- These learners are identified as having a reading age above twelve years. (At about twelve many children are entering Secondary School in New Zealand. Unfortunately this does not necessarily mean they are reading at a twelve-year level).
- A formal spelling programme is not really needed for these learners who learn words easily, and have few spelling mistakes in their writing. They should be applying writing mechanics effortlessly. (e.g. capitals, punctuation, and spelling).
- They can use the computer competently and almost exclusively for their writing.

STAGE FIVE: TEACHER ACTION

The teacher needs to be relaxed enough to allow this kind of learner to take control of the areas in the curriculum they want to personally explore, using the internet to discover knowledge.

Plan carefully to marry the student's interests and skills to the curriculum where necessary. Include the student in this planning. Facilitate the emergence of an individualized self-selected programme, with self-set goals and self-evaluations of how well they have achieved these goals. They should be given time, space and resources to do this. The internet is the place they should be exploring, but with specific goals in mind they have shared with their teacher.

They should study the history or origin of interesting words *such as desperado, digit, festival, vocation, radar, jeep, video, astronaut, backlash* and perhaps report back to the class. This leads them into vast fields of knowledge.

They need to become very familiar with all genre types in order to see the full possibilities for creative communication. Studying excellence in the communication skills of other writers/film makers/ photographers/poets/ artists etc and how it is judged, is the input needed. They need opportunity to practice various genre within and outside the context of the curriculum.

They should be reading and studying the use of metaphor, simile and alliteration in quality creative writing.

Set up opportunity to share with the class (publish) new knowledge they are exploring.

Vocabulary needs constant extension over multiple subject areas. A wide vocabulary allows for better thinking skills.

They need opportunity and encouragement to read widely in order to be introduced to new words in context. They need time to extend their reading independently, as this alone will help their writing.

Expect them to recognize and correct errors and places for improvements. Expect them to proof read their work to check for spelling errors and overworked words. They should be making use of all the opportunities offered by creative publishing programmes with computers. They should be exploring more and more the full scope of publishing on the computer. They can use this to indicate to the teacher changes they have made to their writing to improve it. Celebrate growing precision in their writing.

Have lots of ideas and resources available to help extend and inspire them and also give them practice in using their growing knowledge and skills (see appendix).

Teach students how to use graphic organizers, mind maps and idea maps to build structure into their narrative writing tasks.

They need motivation to maintain a spelling 'conscience' and be committed towards excellence. This type of learner often learns just by being aware of the mistake they have made. If they do decide to stay with a spelling notebook of words to be mastered, words included should be self-selected from those spelled wrongly, and tested only once by their peers perhaps.

Punctuation still needs to be monitored so that finer meanings can be incorporated into their writing. They should know the full scope of how punctuation works (see appendix). The internet will answer any questions they may have on this subject.

The teacher still needs to closely examine the scope and breadth of the genre they are exploring and set up fewer but more in depth conferences with them to determine areas in which improvement and extension can be structured. Students need opportunity and freedom to focus for extended periods of time: e.g. they may decide poetry is for them and spend weeks on becoming a fine poet.

The teacher should source resources that are good examples of what the learner needs to develop/study.

Enrichment activities should be provided for practice of new skills and to introduce new knowledge. A spelling extension list is provided in the appendix, if needed.

They could proof read the work of children at lower levels, and suggest substitutes for overworked words such as *awful, funny, scared, pretty, good, glad, go*

Buddy up with less competent spellers and help with testing words and graph progress, (words learned against time)

Make word charts for the classroom; synonyms, antonyms, homonyms, contractions and abbreviations

They can create slogans and titles for class bulletin boards, and create advertisements manipulating language to achieve a specific purpose.

Construct crossword puzzles for lower level children on class topics.

Play scrabble and anagram word games: Create riddles for others to be answered with words from a list

The student is probably into secondary school now. At this stage they are on the way to become independent learners able to read and write competently enough to take control of the whole educational process with the teacher taking on the role of facilitator.

There is still much to learn (how to write essays, poetry, and how to communicate through art, film, photography, internet communications etc.), but this book does not address this. The internet will provide much guidance at this level.

This text reads bottom to top and is mirrored (*come and get some hot chocolate*) It is also written entirely in capitals which may indicate the child is insecure with lower case letters.

Goals for the child should be set accordingly.

SPECIAL NEEDS OF LOW ACHIEVERS

This text reads bottom to top and is mirrored (*come and get hot chocolate*).
It is also written entirely in capitals which may indicate the child
is insecure with lower case letters

- Students who are low achievers and have special needs will have difficulty in learning and retaining words at their level. They are often low achievers in other areas of the language arts such as reading and oral language. The sample above does not indicate special needs. (Sometimes directionality reverses in the brain temporarily. Left to right progress is a training process that is merely cultural and is not necessarily natural to every child).

- They often lose motivation when they experience multiple problems with text, such as reversals, inversions, poor vision or poor hearing etc.
- They may not be pronouncing words properly. Poor pronunciation is often the cause of spelling errors.
- They may need a high input/output of language and need to work in social groups that allow and encourage this for everyone.
- They need close supervision to keep them on task and to guide them. They need lots of positive reinforcement

LOW ACHIEVERS: TEACHER ACTION

Success for the learner is of major importance and should be pursued slowly, purposefully and closely related to needs.

Build favourable attitudes and good study habits by ensuring:
- Learning tasks focus on specific needs.
- They have access to lots of very easy reading material that is fun and based on repetition, rhyme and word families.(Dr Seuss books are ideal and fun for everybody). Read lots of word family lists that categorize words according to some structural element: For example, search in their reading for words that have *ing* endings, or have *er* (as in *her*) in them. It is important to accept all attempts, but if mistakes persist in writing, check mistakes in reading are not being made for the same reason. For example, it is difficult to detect which end of a word the child is focussing on when trying to figure out words.
- Spelling needs to be words they can easily read and presented in families that are based on patterns. Reduce the number to be learned to no more than the learner feels they can successfully manage. Let the child have some input into this decision.
- Aim for over-learning and revision to ensure words go into the long term memory. Progress will be slower but it is up to the teacher to ensure that it is secure.
- Build in buddy or partner support and reward both of them when objectives are achieved.

Supervise these children closely either through a buddy partnership, a teacher aide, or setting aside time regularly during the day. Ensure they are not in group work that ignores their input or leaves them behind. If they are put into group work, the other children should be taught they are responsible for the progress of all within their group, not just a few.

Use computers for fun activities that revise, are non-threatening, self correcting and amusing.

Give more than the usual amount of time to oral discussion around words to make certain the meanings are known.

Pay particular attention to pronunciation, making certain the pupil can pronounce each word properly.

Study how they are writing the word and you will often find a mispronunciation or a hearing problem that is difficult to pick up otherwise.

Give practice in pronouncing these commonly mispronounced words:
and/an, hair/hear, third, today, Saturday, hundred, thirteen/thirty, fourteen/forty, fifteen/fifty, sixteen/ sixty, pull/bull, seventeen/seventy, eighteen/eighty, nineteen/ninety, kept, brought/bought, been/being, library

Strengthen the learner's visual perception and discrimination through appropriate exercises and activities that are hands-on and multi sensory. For example, strengthen the learner's images of words in his memory by tagging the words with appropriate pictures, and by using colour, texture, pattern etc. The student often enjoys creating these visual images to go with words.

There are many activities and games on the computer for word picture matching, early mastery of letter-sound relationships, and language learning. HooplaKidz and @DarlyndaMiktuk are very good sites.

Clap word that have multi-syllables, then write them in a way that identifies the syllable sounds: *e.g. un-der-stand-ing.*

Colour or circle syllables in words,

Fit words into outlined word shapes

Trace the letter or word's form with a finger in a sand tray, or a wet finger on a chalk-board.

For younger learners, use sand-paper letter shapes.

Provide listening skills practice in auditory discrimination of sounds. (see appendix)

Note any bad habits learners may have developed. Discuss with the student. They need to know about these and be aware of when they are slipping back into them.

Set simple goals in consultation with each learner and reward efforts to achieve them.

Shared reading needs a big emphasis with careful explanation of meanings of words that we often take for granted. Tape-assisted reading and computer sites that are focussed on language learning is another way to get language mileage into a learner who may have had restricted access to words. When you read a story to the class, record it and give it to the learner to take home with the book so it can be revisited.

TECHNOLOGY USE

It is only four years since the iPad was invented. They are flooding into homes and schools. This is beacause in some cases it it cheaper than teachers. Learners love them as they are much more fun than watching and listening to a teacher; furthermore knowlege, in many forms is at their fingertips.

But where will hi-tech classrooms lead our students? Is it good for them? Will it produce smarter kids? The jury is out on that. It is interesting that executives in Silicon Valley are putting their children into Waldof Schools that do not embrace this technology. Why? They invented it. Do they know something the rest of the world doesn't? Apparently they are worried about recent reserch that indicates that long exposure to the light emitting from computer screens affects ability to remember, reshapes neural pathways and damages ability to concentrate. Also one wouldn't argue that this form of learning inhibits creativity, movement, human interactions, and attention span and distract learners as they surf aimlessly through the ethers. They can look like they are doing great things but in actual fact are filling in time and amusing themselves.

On the plus side teachers know that computers and i-Pads can show and explain, give examples, impart information, cause students to learn something, revise and revisit learning, (and have fun and games at the same time). All this can be done by a good teacher too, who, while they are at it, will guide, empower. inspire, enlighten, illuminate, give moral and social instruction, and be a trusted advisor.

So where to from here? It is imperative that teachers and schools should have a clearer vision of the possible future needs of society before they embark on this journey.

What is it to be ? Computers? Teachers? or both? It comes down to deciding why schools exist.

It could be argued that learners come to school to lcarn what they dont know and what they cant learn from their parents. Parents and societies impart cultural knowlledge such as tying shoe laces, eating healthily, dressing yourself, road rules etc. But schools offer academic knowledge inparted by specialists in their subject areas.

Academic knowledge is what makes learners intelligent. Academic institutions such as universities and polytechnics set out to teach learners to criticize, judge, and search for deeper meanings and truths. Can we develop those skills using technology? Probably we will, but we wont find it without being able to read and write well, think creatively, and without moving into fields previously unexplored and not on the internet yet. This is where the future is.

To find a way forward, teachers, schools and government need a cohesive plan. This plan, framed by a clear and courageous vision of the future, may have to encourage and reward teachers who let go some traditional practices and embrace different methods of teaching that actively encourage students to:

- reframe problems
- be creative in finding solutions to problems
- collaborate with others
- lead by influence and good communication skills
- show initiative and entrepreneurship
- be agile and adaptable
- analyse and synthesize information
- use their imaginations
- But, most of all, particularly if they are going to undertake academic learning, they must have effective oral and written communication skills

We must remember that technology is only a part of the overall picture, not the big picture, particularly in elementary schools. And it is already revealing it has some dangers attached. We must tread carefully in case we throw the baby out with the bathwater and end up with students who are no better educated than they were before the invention of the iPad and laptops. That has happened too much in the past when innovation was thrust into schools too fast and without good research and teacher training. Let's learn from our mistakes.

We are back to what this book is all about. It does not decry internet usage, but its key role is always to produce high literacy in all learners and high levels of confidence and skill in the teacher. If internet usage is finely focused on the individual needs of each child, it has much to offer as an adjunct to learning. The fine focus in terms of literacy acquisition can be easily found in this book.

I personally believe that the technological gadgets that are here now, will be, in the future, cleverer and quicker and more fun to use. Teachers are in different places in their knowledge and use of them. They should go at their own pace and not be judged by how many students are using them, but rather by how many students are making good progress according to their individual needs. Teachers should search for the best and most effective learning experiences that not only achieves this, but also creates healthy, independent, creative, optimistic, engaged, life-long learners who will enter the work force and their futures with confidence. Until we are more sure of the long term effects of technology, we must not, in the meantime, fry their brains or endanger their health by over-use of it, particularly in kindergartens and elementary schools.

This book will ensure the teacher remains focused on the student, not the technology.

APPENDIX

This part of the book is a handy reference for teachers once having identified the stage of literacy development the student is functioning at. It is by no means exhaustive and further examples may be found on the internet.

WORD LISTS

Word family lists can be used in several ways:
- they will assist children in developing syllabification skills.
- use them for reading (decoding) practice, particularly in the early stages. This allows the brain to perceive (read) constant elements in certain words. This constancy helps fix these elements in the long term memory for retrieval later when needed for spelling (encoding) a word needed for writing.
- they can be used for testing groups of children at later stages.
- they can be used for word games

ch: chip, chop, chin, child, chap, champ, cheese

Note: Some children cannot hear the difference between the ch and the sh sound, especially combined with the vowel sound i. Make sure they are listening very carefully for the difference, and also make sure they watch your lips when you are modelling how to say them.

sh: she, shed, fish, shoo, shop, cash, sheep, shine, rash, ship, shin, mash, shut, shell, smash, shag, splash, slash

th: the, this, that, these, those, them, then, thank, thick, thin

Note: This is one of the last sounds that children learn to pronounce correctly. They can be ten years of age before some have the physical ability to say "three" instead of "free".

ee (as in *see*): bee, been, tree, cheese, seek, three, need, seed, wee, week, speed, between

oo (as in *zoo*): zoo, shoo, loo, too, moo, coo, boo

y (e): silly, Willy, funny, bunny, sunny, Andy, candy, handy, runnny, Teddy, dolly, lolly, brolly, holly, jolly, Molly, Polly, Billy

Teach the learner to syllabify the words above: e.g. *runny*.
First clap the separate sounds in the word, count how many there are, then write it in syllables (run-ny).
The teacher should model this first.
Most syllables start with a consonant.

y (i): dry, cry, fly, my., sly sky, by, try, sty, fry, shy

ar (as in *car):* car, cars, cart, mart,smart, bar, tar, star, start, starting, far, part, dart, hard, garden, march, park, parking, dark, mark, market

ou (as in *mouse):* our, out, lout,
clout, pout, spout, shout, shouts, shouting, shouted, house, mouse, stout, flour, sprout, about

ow (as in *cow):* cow, how, howl, fowl, bow, now, clown, down, drown, frown, power, brow, brown, flower, tower, shower

 or (as in *for*): for, fort, forty, born, torn, corn, horn, morning , thorn, cord, lord, story, sport, worn, sort

aw (as in *saw*): saw, caw, dawn, jaw, paw, raw, draw, law, slaw, yawn, crawl, hawk, bawl, brawl, trawl, scrawl

all (as in *ball*): fall, wall, ball, hall, tall, stall, mall, small, always, also

ill (as in in *kill*): ill, bill, kill, fill, Jill, pill, spill, smill, till, Billy, silly, until

ell (as in *jelly*): well, bell, fell, jelly, belly, telly, spell, spelling, yell, smell, sell, shell, Nelly, Wellington

oll (as in *doll*): doll, dolly, brolly, jolly, holly, lolly, Molly, Polly, golly

ull (as in *bull):* dull, hull, bull, pull, pulley, full

er (as in *her*): her, herd, germ, dinner, sinner, kerb, winner, spinner, herb, ever, never, term, fern

ir (as in *bird*): bird, third, stir, thirteen, thirty, girl, first, shirt, twirl, thirsty, skirt, swirl, dirty, sir, whirl

Note: With consonant blends it is much easier to work them out in associaton with the vowel(as suggested with single consonants.
Help the learner by covering up the first letter of the blend, work out the word, then add the first letter. e.g. kirt -skirt, rather than sk-irt.

ur (as in *nurse*): curly, churn, fur, furry, nurse, hurt, hurting, purse, burn, burning, turn, turning, Saturday, turtle, Thursday, purple

oy (as in *boy*): boy, joy, Roy, toy, royal, loyal, oyster

oi (as in *oil*): oil, oily, boil, coil, foil, hoist, join, coin, loiter, joiner, spoil, choice

The following lists are a good opportunity to revise the vowel sounds which often give trouble, specially for children with hearing problems or speakers of English as a second language.

ink, ank, unk: sink, sank, sunk, rink, rank, bunk, link, lank, dunk, brink, tank, chunk, blink, blank, hunk, think, thank, junk, drink, drank, drunk, stink, yank, slink, bank

ack, uck, eck, ock, ick: back, black, lack, slack, rack, track, tack, track, Mack, smack, pack, Jack, jacket, packet, snack, slack. dock, lock, locket, rock, crock, rocket, knock, docket, frock, mock, sprocket, flock, knocker, pocket, chocolate, sock, doctor, soccer peck, speck, speckle, deck, freckle, neck, check, checker lick, click, tick, stick, sticker, sticky, Ricky, trick, trickle, tricky, pick pickle, prick, brick, Dick, flick, flicker, slick, slick, sick, nick, quick, quicker, quickest, wick, wicket, thick, snicker, kick, Mick, Mickey buck, duck, duckling, chuck, rick, truck, muck, knuckle,bucket

ight: light, slight, flight, right, bright, fight, tight, might, night

SILENT LETTERS

Stage 2

	sit/site
	kit/kite
bid/bide	*trip/tripe*
rid / ride	*at/ate*
rod/rode	*pal/pale*
pin/pine	*bit /bite*
win/wine	*man/mane*
did/died	*pan/pane*
ran/rain	*Tim/time*
pip /pipe	*lid/lied*
rip/ripe	

USEFUL SPELLING RULES

Stage 1-2

a, e, i, o, u are vowels. All other letters in the alphabet are consonants, except *y* which can be both.

a is used before words that begin with a consonant: e.g. *a bat, a tiger, a man, a house* etc.

an is used before words that begin with vowels: e.g. *an indian, an egg,   an apple, an aunt, an umbrella, an old hat*

To show the present tense of most verbs such as *ride*, (as in *I am riding to school in the bus)*, you just add *ing*

Stage 2-3

To words that end in *e*, leave the *e* off before adding *ing:* e.g.,
come/coming
dance/dancing
Exceptions:
see/seeing
be/being
tie/tying

Stage 2-3

To words that end with a single consonant that are preceded by a single vowel, double the consonant and then add *-ing: e.g.*
knit/knitting
swim/swimming
stir/stirring
get/getting
hop/hopping
stop/stopping

SYLLABIFICATION

Stage 2-3

There are no set rules for syllabification.

Note: The learner has to hear the sounds separately in a word. Students should be given practice at listening first, then clapping the sounds, saying them, then try to write the word.

To begin with, choose simple syllables. As a general rule;

Every syllable has a vowel and mostly begin with a consonant, (unless they are prepositions)

riv-er	*pun-ish*	*hap-py*
for-get	*re-turn*	*rat-tle*
sum-mer	*stir-ring*	*bun-dle*
for-bid	*dai-sy*	*skid-ding*
hil-ly	*pep-per*	*cree-ping*
fun-ny	*rub-ber*	*craw-ling*
sud-den	*rag-ged*	*stic-king*
car-pet	*pi-per*	*un-der-stand*
un-less	*cle-ver*	*hel-i-cop-ter*
can-not	*Ea-ster*	
go-ing	*ca-mel*	
win-ter	*vi-sit*	
No-vem-ber	*ti-ger*	
Sep-tem-ber	*trac-tor*	
Fri-day	*chur-ches*	
Sa-tur-day	*spi-der*	
him-self	*a-loud*	
pol-ish	*flow-er*	
sel-fish	*tic-ket*	
sud-den-ly	*but-ter-fly*	
a-round	*an-y-bo-dy*	
a-go	*un-ab-le*	
a-like	*kit-chen*	

SINGULARS AND PLURALS

Stage 1

Usually -s is added to make a singular noun plural e.g. *hat/hats*

Stage 2-3

Add -es if the noun already ends in *s, o, ch, x, sh* : e.g.-
box/boxes
fox/foxes
brush/brushes
gas /gases
glass/glasses
watch/watches
dress/dresses
bus/buses
match/matches
peach/ peaches
branch/branches
patch/ patches
church/churches
thrush/thrushes
class classes
ditch/ditches

If the word ends in -*f,* the *f* changes to *v* and then add *es*: e.g.
calf/calves
half/halves
leaf/leaves
loaf/loaves
shelf/shelves
thief/thieves
wolf/wolves
knife/knives
life/lives
glove/gloves
Exceptions:
dwarf / dwarfs
chief /chiefs

reef / reefs
roof / roofs
hoof / hoofs / hooves

If the word ends in -o, add-es: e.g
cargo/cargoes
echo/echoes
hero/heroes
Negro/Negroes
potato/potatoes
tomato/ tomatoes
Exceptions:
banjo/banjos
piano/pianos
solo/ solos

PLURALS ENDING IN -y

Stage 3-4

To make a plural of nouns or verbs that end in *-y* and have a consonant before the *-y*, change the *y* to *i* and add *-es* or *-ed: e.g.*
army/armies
fairy/fairies
story/stories
daisy/daisies
city/cities
lily/lilies
party/parties
cherry/cherries
lady/ladies
sky/skies
baby/babies
spy/spies
berry/berries
hurry/hurries/hurried
worry/worries/worried
bury/buries/buried
carry/carries/carried
try/tries/tried
reply/replies/ tried
pity/pities/pitied
dry/dries/dried
hurry/hurries/hurried
empty/empties/emptied

marry/marries/married
tidy/tidies/tidied
Exceptions:
valley/valleys

UNUSUAL PLURALS

child/children
foot/feet
goose/geese
man/men
mouse/mice
ox/oxen
tooth/teeth
woman/women
cupful/cupfuls
hanger-on/hangers-on
spoonful/spoonsful
brother/brothers/brethren
cloth/cloths/clothes
die/dies/dice
fish/fish/fishes
genius/geniuses/genii
pea/peas/pease
dozen/dozen/dozens
cannon/cannon
cod/cod
deer/deer
grouse/grouse
salmon/salmon
sheep/sheep
swine/swine
trout/trout
brother-in law/brothers-in-law
son-in-law/sons-in-law
by-law/by-laws
by-way/by-ways
maid-of-honour/maids-of-honour
man-of-war/men-of-war
mouse-trap/mouse-traps
passer-by/passers-by

Some words have no singular: e.g.
bellows, billiards, gallows, measles, pincers, pliers, scissors, shears, spectacles, thanks, tidings, tongs, trousers, tweezers, victuals

PUNCTUATION

FULL STOP

Stage 1-2

Full stops go at the end of a sentence: *This is the way to do it.*

Stage 3-5

Full stops are used for shortened forms of words when the shortened form consists of the first letter and another letter or letters, but not the last letter. e.g.

Jan. (January)
Melb. (Melbourne)
Tele. (Telephone)
Pres. (President)
Lic. (Licence)
Fri. Friday)
pop. (population)
cent. (century)

The following abbreviations do not need a full stop, because both the first letter and the last letter of the word is used

Mr
Mrs
St
Rd
Ave
Rly (Railway)
Stn (Station)
Ltd (Limited)
Pty (Proprietary)
Dr (Doctor)
Jr (Junior)
Sr (Senior)

In metric abbreviations, full stops are never used at the end and the letter -s is never used to form plurals: e.g.

m: metre(s)

km/kilometre

g: grams

l: litre

km/h: kilometres per hour

Abbreviations for ante meridian and post meridian are written either as *a.m* or *am* and *p.m* or *pm*. Both are correct.

Abbreviations made up of capital letters are written without full stops: e.g.

BBC

AO

GPO

ACT

NZ

USA

RSPCA

Words formed from initials (acronyms), are written without full stops: e.g.

scuba (self contaiined underwater breathing apparatus)

radar (radio detecting and ranging)

NATO (North Atlantic Treaty Organization)

Full stops should not be used in titles and headings: e.g. newspaper stories, film and book titles.

Full stops are used to show decimal places: e.g.

6.2

0.001

78.325

CAPITALS

Stage 1-2

Capitals
- begin sentences: e.g. *This is my hat.*
- begin special names: e.g. *It is Sunday the first of May*
- are used for the word *I. e.g. I am at school.*

Stage 2-3

Capitals

- begin direct speech: e.g. *She shouted, "Go!"*
- sometimes begin lines of poetry: e.g
  Ride a cock-horse
  To Banbury Cross."
- write the important names of organizations: e.g
  Raglan Fishing Club,
  Naike Primary School
  Campervan Organization
- are used for the important words in the titles of books, such as TV shows, plays, songs, etc:
  e.g.
  Snow White and the Seven Dwarfs, Scooby Doo, Singing in the Rain, God of Nations

Stage 3-4

Capitals

- are used for adjectives formed from proper nouns: e.g
  Australian, Maori, English
- are used for people's titles: e.g.
  President Bush
  Archbishop Gregory
  Sergeant Johns
  Queen Elizabeth 11
  Chairman Yang

Stage 4-5

Capitals

- begin words of exclamation:e.g. *Stop!*
- begin words He, Him, His, if they refer to God or some other deity
- begin a heading: e.g
  Drowning claims a life
  Girl saves cat
- are not used for the seasons, (spring, summer, autumn, winter, and are not used for school subjects (science, handwriting, reading).
- are used for languages: e.g.
  Russian Chinese

QUESTION MARK

Stage 1-2

Question marks go at the end of a question. *How are you today?*

EXCLAMATION MARK

Stage 3-5

Exclamation marks
- show extreme surprise, disbelief, indignation, or emotion. It replaces a full stop at the end of an exclamatory sentence. e.g.
  He was the tallest man in the world!
  I just couldn't believe my eyes!
  Go!
  I was so overcome by the scene I couldn't talk!
  She was so looking forward to the meal: It turned out to be awful!
- are used with a greeting or words called out to a one or a group: e.g.
  Happy birthday to you!
  Encore!
  Great work kids!
  Order in the court!

Note: Sometimes a sentence looks like a question but is more like an exclamation. If no answer is expected it can probably be regarded as an exclamation.

  I mean to say: What sort of person would do a thing like that!
  How stupid can I get!

COMMA

Commas mark very short pauses in reading. Their basic purpose is to make the meaning of a passage quite clear and ensure there is no misunderstanding.

Commas should not be used if they interrupt the natural flow of language.

Stage 1

Commas should be used for a pause in a sentence. e.g. *I was so overcome with grief, I burst into tears.*

Stage 2

Use commas between words in a list of things except before *and*

  We picked, apples, oranges, plums and peaches.

Stage 3-5

Commas
- are placed after the speaker in a conversation or after the direct speech: e.g.
  "I'm over here," said John.

John said, "How are you?
- mark off the part of the sentence that puts the speech in its setting, but is not actually part of the direct speech. e.g.
"Many old settlers," the teacher began, "came here first to search for gold."
"I am hear to help you," said the coach.

Stage 4-5

Commas
- separate clauses that are not essential to a subject, but add to it in some way: e.g. *The kiwi, which is an unusual bird, is the emblem of New Zealand.*
- mark off introductory phrases and clauses: e.g.
Every second day during winter, she cleaned out the grate.
After reaching the swing bridge, the hunter began to climb the steep hill.
- mark off phrases that come between the subject and the verb in a sentence. e.g.
Helen Clarke, during the election, spoke to the media on the subject of law and order.
- separate clauses that are fairly long and have different subjects. e.g.
The littlle girl stayed in bed till her parents woke up, but she was bored and wanted to get up.
- mark off words, phrases and clauses that are "asides" from the main sentence. e.g.
I want you two children, Billy and Sally, to go down to the shed to get some balls.
- separate adjectives when the meaning would not be clear without them. e.g.
It was a very pretty, larg-leafed plant.
The children raced along the yellow, hot, sandy, shell -sprinkled beach.
- separate numbers. e.g.
John's scores in the tests were 86, 21, 42, and 3.
- should not be used in dates. e.g *17 July 2002* or in setting out large numbers. Modern practice runs numerals together up to 9999, and thereafter leaves a small space between groups of three numerals. e.g.
4768
10 234
243 651
5 246 468
- should not be used in setting out an address: e.g.
Mr Tony Kissingha
316 Waterfall Road
Wellington

APOSTROPHE

Stage 2-4

An apostrophe is used
- when letters have been left out to shorten a word: e.g. in contractions such as
isn't / is not

we've / we have
couldn't / could not,

Note: don't confuse the contraction "it's" (meaning "it is" with the possessive pronoun its.e.g.

It's the first day of spring
The dog is chewing its bone.

Stage 3-4

Use apostrophes
- when ownership needs to be shown: e.g.
  Mary's bag
  cat's whiskers

Stage 4-5

Use apostrophes
- to form the possessive of a plural noun that already ends in *-s*, e.g.
  the girls' swing set (the swing set belonging to the girls)
  the students' projects (the projects belonging to the students)
  the Johnsons' house (the house belonging to the Johnsons)

If the plural noun does not end in *-s*, add an apostrophe plus *-s*: e.g.

the women's conference (the conference belonging to the women)
the children's toys (the toys belonging to the children)
the men's training camp (the training camp belonging to the men)

When two or more nouns possess the same thing, add an apostrophe plus *-s* to the last noun listed: e.g.
Jodie, Jane and Brett 's box of biscuits.
Emma and Teresa"s school project (Emma and Teresa worked together on the same project)

With possessive pronouns that already show ownership, it's not necessary to add an apostrophe: e.g.
yours, his, hers, its, ours

However, we do add an apostrophe plus *-s* to form the possessive of some indefinite pronouns: e.g.
anybody's guess
one's personal responsibility
somebody's wallet

Generally, do not use an apostrophe to form a plural. Use only an *-s* (or an *-es*) without an apostrophe to form the plurals of nouns, (including dates, acronyms, and family names): e.g.
Gold prices were booming in the 1990s.
The tax advantages offered by secondary homes make them attractive investments.
The Johnsons have sold all of their DVDs.

To avoid confusion, we may occasionally need to use apostrophes to indicate the plural forms of certain letters and expressions that are not commonly found in the plural: e.g.

> *Mind your p's and q's.*
> *Let's do this without any if's, and's, or but's.*

QUOTATION MARKS

The primary function of quotation marks is to identify exact language (either spoken or written) that has come from somebody else.

Quotation marks can also be used to designate speech acts in fiction and sometimes poetry. It may be of interest that usage rules for quotation marks vary in other countries.

Stage 2-3

Learners should identify pairs of quotation marks in their reading and discuss why they may have been used. Focus on quotation marks for direct speech.

Students could transfer small sections of a play genre into direct speech for practice or particularly practice usage by writing a conversation. Each time a new person speaks a new paragraph is started and it may even be just one word. e.g.

> *"I am the best football player in the school," Alan boasted.*
> *"What?"*

They should understand that the full stop, question mark or comma comes before the final quotation mark.

Stage 4

Students should dentify direct quotes in their reading. Sometimes they are indicated by only one quotation mark at the beginning and end of the quote.

They should practice direct quotes in their writing. e.g. *Mr Smith, who was the teacher, said with a smile on his face, 'I am pleased to announce that John has won the film making competition."*

Capitalize the first letter of a direct quote when the quoted material is a complete sentence.

Stage 5

Quotation marks can be problematic and the use of the internet will show that this is an area tied up with plagiarism when quoting other's work. At this level, it would be useful to direct students to the internet to study and practice quotation marks.

PARAGRAPHING SKILLS

The basic rule of thumb with paragraphing is to keep one idea to one paragraph. If the writer begins to transition into a new idea, it belongs in a new paragraph. There are some simple ways to tell if one is on the same topic or a new one. The writer can have one idea and several bits of supporting evidence within a single paragraph. Or they can also have several points in a single paragraph as long as they relate to the overall topic of the paragraph. If the single points start to get long, then perhaps elaborating on each of them and placing them in their own paragraphs is the route to go.

Stage 3-4

Go back into shared reading and study and discuss how and why writers use paragraphs. Do not expect students to use paragraphing in their writing yet. But,
- Identify where a paragraph starts and finishes.
- Know what a paragraph is (a collection of related sentences dealing with a single topic. It may also be a piece of direct speech in a conversation. Each time a new person talks it is begun as a new paragraph).
- Identify why the author has begun a new paragraph in a general way. (A new idea or topic is being introduced which takes the story forward and will assist the reader in following a piece of writing).
- Identify the main topic sentence in a paragtaph.
- Speech marks indicate when a person is talking. When a new person talks then a new paragraph is also started.

Stage 5

A topic sentence indicates in a general way what the paragraph is dealing with. Although not all paragraphs have clear-cut topic sentences, they can occur anywhere in the paragraph (the first sentence, the last sentence, or somewhere in the middle), A good general rule for less experienced writers, (although it is not the only way to do it) is to put the topic sentence near the beginning of the paragraph. Regardless of whether one should include an explicit topic sentence or not, one should be able to easily summarize what the paragraph is about.

Go back into the student's reading to:
- Identify topic sentences in each paragraph. Write a summary of the piece of writing once having done this.
- Practice paragraphing skills. This can be done when preparing for speeches or class debates. As part of this, practice writing good introductory and conclusion paragraphs and when contrasting information or ideas..

COLON

The colon marks a pause or separation not quite as definite as that indicated by a full stop.

Stage 5

Colons are used:
- to introduce an explanation or enlargement of what comes after the colon: e.g. to introduce a list
  The teacher said the clothes needed for the trip were: track suits, rain jacket, sturdy shoes, two pairs of socks,   and a woolly hat.
  These are the behaviours exhibited by bullies: hitting, nudging, name-calling, put-downs and aggressive body language.
  To make a milk shake you will need: milk, flavouring, ice cream and sugar.
- to introduce a quotation or reported speech: e.g.
  The teacher shouted loudly: " Please line up in your teams."
  Keats wrote: "Season of mists and mellow fruitfulness."
- to introduce a question:e.g.
  What flowers will you plant in your garden: pansies? nemesia? roses?
  We must ask ourselves this: How much am I prepared to give up to achieve this goal?
  Do not go near that dangerous cliff: otherwise you may slip, fall and be killed.
- to show ratios or proportion: For example,
  1 : 100
  1 : 25
- after the names in a script or play:e.g.
  John: I won't go there ever again.
  Mum: Well I am pleased that you have come to that conclusion
  Father: You are beginning to make good decisions for yourself.

SEMICOLON

Stage 5

This is a difficult form of punctuation to master.

To look at it, the semi colon is a combination of a comma and a full stop. This indicates its usage. When one wants to form a bond between two statements, (typically when they are related or they contrast with one another), use a semicolon.

Semicolons are used
- to separate independent clauses that could stand alone, (each being a sentence,) but they are closely connected in meaning: e.g.
  My dog has a curly coat: it does not shed all over the house.
- If one connects the two statements with a comma, one can use *but* instead of a semi-colon.
  e.g. *"My dog has a curly coat, but it does not shed all over the house.*
- if you need to make a list of items that are separated by a comma: e.g.
  I travelled to Auckland, New Zealand; Sydney, Australia; and Paris, France.

Do not use it with conjunctions such as *" and, but, or, nor, for, so, yet"* Use a comma instead

TROUBLESOME WORDS

These words may require direct testing/teaching. Pay particular attention to the learner gaining visual impressions (memory) of them. They are good words to have team competitions with.

lose (opposite of win)	*enough*	*women*	*your, you're*
loose (not tight)	*friend*	*listen*	*it's(possession)*
ache	*guess*	*build*	*its (it is)*
across	*heard*	*huge*	*definitely*
again	*one*	*sign*	*effect (a noun)*
afraid	*school*	*people*	*affect (a verb)*
already	*sure*	*earth*	*weather (snow, rain,*
among	*they*	*usual*	*etc.)*
any	*tonight*	*laugh*	*whether*
colour	*thought, bought,*	*buy*	*a lot (two words)*
could, would, should	*brought, (bring)*	*view*	*then (used for time)*
cousin	*very*	*quite*	*than (used for*
dead	*wait*	*quiet*	*comparison)*
decide	*want*	*question*	
does	*were*	*answer*	
doesn't	*when*	*weird*	

HOMONYMS

Homonyms are words that have different meanings and spellings, but share the same pronunciation. These words can be a source of poor comprehension in reading. To teach these words successfully requires that the learners understand all their meanings.

Stage 2-3

ate/eight	*meet/meat*	*some/sum*	*bored/board*
ball/bawl	*rode/road*	*hear/here (can be*	*bough/bow*
blew/blue	*sail/sale*	*confused with "hair")*	*boy/buoy*
dear/deer	*sea/see*	*stare/stair*	*ceiling/sealing*
flower/flour	*son/sun*	*aloud/allowed*	*seller/cellar*
fool/full	*tail/tale*	*beech/beach*	*cheap / cheep*
new/knew	*to/too/two*	*by/bye*	*die/dye*
no/know	*one/won*	*your/your're*	*fore/four/for*
knows/nose	*for/four*	*bare/bear*	*grate/great*

groan/grown
herd/heard
whole/hole
hour/our
knight/night
knot/not
maid / made
mail/male
mist/missed
mane/main
none/nun
pail/pale
pause/paws
plane/plain
ring/wring
seen/scene
sent/scent
reins/rains/reigns
so/sew/sow
seam/seem
reed/read
real/reel
rose/rows
sore/soar
steel/steal
through / threw

root/route
told/tolled
weak/week
waist/waste
wait/weight
would/wood
there/their/they're
wear/ware/where (were)

Stage 4

bale/bail
bell/belle
boar/bore
cereal/serial
check/cheque
coarse/course
cruise/crews
current/currant
desert/dessert
ewe/yew/you
fare/fair
feat/feet
foul/fowl
hale/hail
hare/heir/hair

hire/higher
him/hymn
holy/wholly
leek/leak
flew/flue
mare/mayor
lightening/lightning
loan/lone
lute/loot
site/sight
steak/stake
vale/veil
muscle/mussel
piece/peace
peel/peal
plum/plumb
pores/paws
sole/soul
style/stile
thrown/ throne
time/thyme
praise/preys/prays
vein/vain/vane
right/rite/write/wright
raise/rays/raze

Stage 5

air/heir
aisle/isle
alley/ally
core/corp
council/counsel
gate/gait
draft/draught
faint/feint
gambol/gamble
gilt/guilt
horde/hoard
key/quay
medal/meddle
o'er/ oar/ore
picture/pitcher
peer/pier
plaice/place
practise/practice
principle/principal
prophet/profit
rye/wry
statonery/stationary
tears/tiers

GENDER

Stage 1

papa/mama
Mr./Mrs.
male/female
man/woman
prince/princess
king/queen
husband/wife
brother/sister
boy/girl
father/mother
grandmother /
grandfather

son/daughter

Stage 2

giant/giantess
god/goddess
wizard/witch
tiger/tigress
lion/lioness
hunter / huntress
ogre/ogress
master/mistress

lad/lass
gentleman/lady
uncle/aunt
nephew/niece
bridegroom/bride
waiter/waitress
bull/cow
dog/bitch
drake/duck
billy-goat/nanny-goat
post-man/postwoman

Stage 3

actor/actress
author/authoress
emperor/empress
conductor/conductress
host/hostess
murderer/murderess
enchanted /enchantress
mayor/mayoress
lord/lady
manager/manageress

poet/poetess
sir/madam
shephed/shepherdess
sorcerer/sorceress
boar/sow
buck/doe
bullock/heifer
cock/hen
colt/ illy
gander/goose
stallion/mare
ram/ewe
step-mother/step-father
step-son/step-daughter

Stage 4

baron/baroness
count/countess
duke/duchess
heir/heiress
maid-servant/
man-servant
Jew/Jewess
Negro/Negress
priest/priestess
bachelor/spinster
brave/squaw
friar/nun

monk/nun
hero/heroine
steward/stewardess
tailor/ tailoress
tutor/governess
widow/widower
cob pen (swan)
sire/dam
stag/hind
steer/heifer
buck/doe
landlord/landlady
mother-in-law/
father-in-law

son-in-law/
daughter-in-law

Stage 5

proprietor/proprietrix
executor/executrix
marquis/marchioness
patron/patroness
masseur/masseuse
earl/countess
beau belle
prophet/prophetessg
Sultan/Sultana

COMMON PREFIXES AND THEIR MEANINGS

(This is good extension work for gifted children)

Stage 4-5

a means *on*: e.g. afloat ashore, aloft

a ,ab, abs means *away* or *from*: e.g. avert, absent, abstract

ad, ac, ar means: *to* .e.g. adhere, accept, arrive

ante means *before*: e.g. anteroom, ante-natal

bi, bis means *two, twice*: e.g. bicycle, bisect, biped.

circum means *round*: e.g. circumference, circuit

com means *together*: e.g. competition comfort

contra means *against*: e.g. contrary, contradict

de means *down*. e.g descend, depress

dif, dis means *apart, not*. e.g. different, disagree

ex means *out of*: e.g. exhale, export, extract

fore means *before*: e.g. forecast, foresee

im, in, means *in, into*: e.g. import, include

inter means *between*: e.g. interlude, interrupt.

mis means *wrong*: e.g. mistake, misplace

ob means *against*: e.g. object, obstruction

post means *after*: e.g. postpone, postscript

pre means *before*: e.g. predict, pre-war

pro means *forth*: e.g. proceed, produce

re means *back, again*.e.g return retake, retrace

sub means *under*. e.g. submarine subway

trans means *across*. e.g. transfer, transport

un means *not, without*. e.g. unfit, unknown, unsafe

vice means *instead*.e.g. vice-captain, viceroy, vice-president

COMMON SUFFIXES AND THEIR MEANINGS

Stage 4-5

-able, -ible mean *capable of being*: e.g. *moveable, eatable*

-ain, -an mean *one connected*: e.g. *chaplain, publican*

-ance, -ence mean: *state of* : e.g. *repentence, existence*

-ant means *one who*: e.g. *servant, assistant*

-el, -et, -ette, means *little*: e.g.*satchel, locket, cigarette*

-ess means *the female e*:: e.g. *lioness, goddess*

-fy means *to make*: e.g. *simplify, glorify, purify*

-icle,-sel means *little*: e.g. *icycle, morsel, particle*

-less means *without*: e.g. *careless, merciless*

-ling means *little*: e.g. *duckling, darling,*

-ment means *state of being*: e.g. *merriment, enjoyment*

-ock means *little*: e.g. *hillock,*

-oon, -on means *large*: e.g. *saloon, balloon, flagon*

-ory means *a place for*: e.g. *dormitory, factory*

-ous means *full of*: e.g. *famous, glorious*

WORDS THAT DESCRIBE FEELINGS THAT CHILDREN SHOULD UNDERSTAND

Understanding these words adds immeasurably to comprehension. They are great for impromptu drama activities.

Stage 1

angry, annoyed, afraid, awful, bad, brave, bored, confused, cheerful, caring, clever, disappointed, delighted, excited, eager, friendly, funny, frightened, foolish, grouchy, grumpy, greedy, happy, hurt, interested, ignored, joyful, jealous, kind, keen, loving, lucky, lazy, mad, nice, naughty, nasty, mischievous, noisy, okay, obedient, quiet, pleased, ready, sad, surprised, silly, smiley, scared, shy, sorry, safe, tired, worried, well, yucky

Stage 2

anxious, abandoned, agreeable, bothered, brilliant, confident, calm, curious, cautious, defiant, destructive, determined, disgusted, energetic, encouraged, enthusiastic, embarassed, exhausted, envious, furious, fortunate, forgiving, green with envy, generous, grateful, helpless, honest, horrified, proud, impatient, invisible, jumpy, likable, mixed-up, miserable, marvellous, magical, nervous, neglected, needy, overjoyed, over-the-top, peaceful, playful, question, panic, peaceful, perfect, puzzled, proud, stubborn, satisified, stupid, thankful, tearful, thoughtful, terrific, talkative, timid, tolerant, trusted, uncertain, ugly, unafraid, uncomfortable, useless, weak, yappy,

Stage 3

alarmed, absent minded, awkward, baffled, blue, clumsy, cooperative, considerate, content, disorganized, discouraged, daring, edgy, enraged, frustrated, grief stricken, hopeless, heart-broken, irritated, ignorant, insecure, inspired, knocked down, laid back, light-hearted, lousy, lost, mean miserable, moody, mopey, mistrustful, manipulative, out-of-control, neglected, over-powered, over-stimulated, off, obstinate, peachy, offended, peppy, petty, picky, powerful, powerless, relieved, relaxed, reluctant, reasonable, restful, restive, reassured, snarly, serious, stressed out, tantrumy, troubled, tickled, torn, trustworthy, touched, threatened tolerant, trusted, unruly, uneasy, unruffled, up, unimpressed, unappreciated, undecided, unique, violent, victorious, vacant, wacky, wary, warm, witty, withdrawn, worthless, wronged, willful, wishful, weary, weird, weepy, whiny, worn out, wound up, zapped

Stage 4

affectionate, bashful, bitter, exuberant, devious, depressed, flustered, gullible, honoured, humble, humiliated, irresponsible, indifferent, inadequate, judgmental, meek, modest, mellow, maternal, manipulative, nerdy, noble, neglectful, outraged, obsessive, obligated, peeved, questionable, quivery, respected, resentful, rattled, refreshed, repulsed, rageful, reserved, reactive, remorseful, rebellious, smug, serene, scornful, spiteful, loyal sarcastic, sociable, snarky, secure, sensitive, temperamental, vain, valued, wistful, woeful, youthful, yielding, yearning, zonked, zippy, zestful,

Stage 5

Aggravated, compassionate, detached, expectant, disillusioned, malevolent, leery, lacklustre, labile, melodramatic, nonplussed nonchalant, nauseated, irrational, irked, jaded, jocular, jinxed, naive, pre-occupied, quirky, pensive, petulant, psyched, querulous, patronized, qualified, reactive, rational, sassy,vivacious, vibrant, vital, vexed, volatile, vulnerable,whimsical, xenophobic, zany, zealous, zen,

ENGLISH IDIOMATIC EXPRESSIONS

An idiom is a phrase where the words together have a meaning that is different from the dictionary definitions of the individual words. This makes idioms difficult for learners of English as a second language to comprehend the text.

There are over three thousand common expressions that native English speakers use without thinking but they cause great confusion for learners who are not aware of them.

e.g.
hold your tongue (stop talking)
hold your horses (wait)
scarce as hen's teeth (not easily found)
pull the pin (give up)
born on the wrong side of the tracks (of low social status)
pick of the litter (the best one in the group)
spoilt for choice (too many options)

There are so many idioms in the English language it is impossible to deal with them here, but they are avilable in special dictionaries and on the internet.

At elementary level, it is enough that the teacher is alert to problems they may cause in comprehension of the text, and explain them to the class within the context being studied.

SPELLING GAMES AND IDEAS FOR FILL-INS

There is a huge range of games and activities on the internet to help consolidate skills. But there is a place for full classroom participation where a few moments can be filled in before recess etc. This also gives opportunity for students of all levels to interact and learn from each other.

TO PRACTICE PLURALS

Have a list of tricky plurals in the classroom or available to each child. One child comes out and challenges the others "Who can spell the word that means more than one knife?" The one who can is chosen becomes the next challenger.

TO PRACTICE ROOT WORDS

Class divided into groups . One child writes a root word on the board. He asks the groups to write neatly and spell correctly on a slip of paper new words with this base: For example, *write/writer/writing/writes/written.*

One point is given for each correctly spelled word. A time limit is put on the task. (The words that have accumulated can be used later for personal sorting by low achievers.)

TO PRACTICE TROUBLESOME WORDS

Divide the class into mixed ability teams each with access to a list of words that are troublesome to spell. They should be graded in difficulty if the teams are of mixed ability. Give them time to learn the level most appropriate to their ability.

The teacher then pronounces the word carefully, puts it in a sentence, then says, "Go". Each member of the team in turn has to run out with the felt pen or chalk (which is like a relay baton), and each write a letter of the word. First relay team to complete it wins 5 points. Second team 4 points. third team 3 points. Team with most points at the end of the game wins.

Divide the class into equal groups. Give each child in each group a number that corresponds to their spelling level. Call out a number and children in that level come out. Then call out three words from their level which they must remember and then write on the board. Tally the number that are incorrectly spelled. The team with the lowest score at the end wins.

TO PRACTICE SYLLABIFICATION

Teacher writes on separate slips of paper each syllable of each word from a list of words. (The complete word is written on the back of the slip of paper. The words might be topic words that are part of a class study that is already on the board for reference).

They are then put in a box that is shaken up.

Divide the class into 2 teams. One member of one team draws a syllable from the box and writes it on the board. each member of the other team has to anticipate the word and write it down. Points are scored according to the number of children in the group who have managed to get the word correct. There is an element of luck because many words may have the same syllable.

The second team then gets to challenge.

Divide the class into teams. Write identical lists of words on the board but not in the same order, one list for each team. Everyone has a chance to study the words, Now erase a letter or syllable from each word. On saying, "Go" each member of each team runs out and has a turn putting in a missing letter in one word. The first team finished their list wins.

PRACTICE LISTENING FOR FIRST AND LAST LETTER OF A WORD

One child says a word then spells it. The next child has to spell a word that begins with the last letter of the word that has been spelled. No word can be used twice.

HOW TO LEARN A LETTER OR WORD

Very young students should:
- search for it in their reading
- illustrate it with a picture: e.g 'b' for a 'banana'.
- trace over the teacher's sample
- Insert it into a personalized picture dictionary.
- paint over it with a finger dipped in paint
- write with a wet finger on a blackboard
- collage over it with sand, shells, paper dots etc
- run/hop around the shape the teacher has chalked on the pavement

Older students should now understand the difference between their short and long term memory and that the following activities can help put it into the latter.
- record the sentence or context that they have discovered it in. Look up a simple dictionary to clarify its meaning. Use it in a sentence of their own.
- copy the word onto a piece of paper. Check to see if it is right. If not, carefully copy it again, and trace over it with a different coloured penci. Fold it over and rewrite/check etc.
- close eyes and pretend to write it in the sky
- return to it the next day and revise at least twice.

FOR THE TEACHER

Sometimes to take a first step into unknown territory is scary. I have experienced this myself. So to make it easier here is a way to start.

Read this book

Start by analysing a child's piece of unassisted writing and list all the mistakes. Refer back to the child's reading to see where you can feed in what is needed from their readiing. e.g: If the child is not starting a sentence with a capital, are they stopping and waiting when they see this in their reading? (. , ! ?) . Check their reading to establish this. If they aren't, teach them to do this and list as a goal in their writing books.

  1.   *I will stop and wait when I see this . , ? ! in my reading*

(To do this , easy reading must be chosen because, if it is difficult, they will stop to work out the word). They must put some of these stops into their own writing to tell you where to stop when you read it, so you have two goals now.

  2.   *I will put in a full stop, comma, exclamation mark or a question mark when I want the reader of my writing to stop and wait.*

Use shared reading to learn the usage of these punctuation marks. Can the child identify an exclamation, a question or a place to stop but are not finished yet ? (This can be done with a group of children with similar needs).

Only when they know where to put in full stops in their writing can you get to putting in capitals at the start of new sentences.

  3.   *I will start my sentences with a capital letter.*

You will be surprised to find the child's comprehension of their reading soars so they enjoy it more, it is easier to read, and their written language is better. etc. You are on your way, and the child's reading is starting to improve.

Now you can refer to the stage the child is at in this book to see what is appropriate to teach about capital letters, (appendix), or go back to that piece of unassisted writing and select another item to work on. e.g spelling. If they are writing his as hes, make sure they are saying the vowel sounds properly. Give them a list of words in a note book to read, (not spell,) saying the sounds correctly. When they can do this, have them select a few to learn, letting them choose how many for a goal:

4.   *I will learn the difference between the e and i sound.*

Find other children in the class with the same problems (by analysing their writing), and group them.

Work with one child or a group, until you are confident enough to extend it to other children. Keep the samples of work, date them, and record in your work plans what you are working on. Record also their reading ages, (but you have probably already done this).

Decide if this book has something to offer.

Go back and read the book again. Good luck.

END NOTES

1   I have written a book, awaiting publication, on this topic. It explores this negation of voice within my own life story.

2   Using this approach, I saw the need for, and designed, another resource that was lacking in schools, *Accelerated Alphabet Learning*. This is a programme covering most curriculum areas for the first two years of schooling, based upon a uniquely designed alphabet. It has been referred to in this book, as an extra resource that deepens knowledge at this early stage of literacy acquisition, (where reading and understanding the alphabet is crucial for writing.) It is particularly suitable for children with forms of dyslexia.

3   First, they need to ensure the specialist vocabulary of their subject area is understood and check if it is used in their assignments. Then they need to select a few goals based on the structure of this book and what needs work. This could be done by the English specialist teacher. If all secondary teachers are on the same page with regards goals for the learner, progress will continue class to class, and students are less likely to drop out in frustration. Reading/writing skills should not be neglected because the student is learning maths for example.

4   In early childhood classrooms, shared reading typically involves a teacher and a large group of children sitting closely together to read and reread carefully selected enlarged texts. Shared reading can also be done effectively with groups. With this instructional technique, students have an opportunity to gradually assume more responsibility for the reading as their skill level and confidence increase. Shared reading also provides a safe learning environment for students to practice the reading behaviours of proficient readers with the support of teacher and peers. Shared reading may focus on needs indicated in assessment data. The text is always chosen by the teacher and must be visible to all students.

5   At birth the language areas of the brain are fully developed, but it is well known that many orphans in institutions, who have their physical but not mental and emotional needs met, often fail to thrive. Little language fed in usually creates developmental delay and often these children fail to catch up.

6   It is interesting that for most infants, hearing is established in the womb and is the only totally developed sense at birth and the last sense one loses at death. Also it has been proven that from birth to three or four years of age, children have brains that can learn multiple languages more successfully than at any other time of life. Is nature not telling us something?

7   A word is a symbol that allows thinking and communication. A block of wood may be a symbol for a car; a paint daub a symbol for a sun; a circle within a circle, a symbol for their mother. The symbols just become more sophisticated as they mature.

8   Picture drawing is a common starting point for psychologists dealing with traumatized children.

9   Children coming to school with some knowledge of rhyming words gained from Nursery Rhymes are said to do better in their reading in the first year at school.

10   They need a reading age of at least seven years before there has been sufficient exposure to print to be able to do this. It is wise not to begin a formal spelling programme until then.
Training in recognizing colour, shape size and number patterns in the first years at school is important if they are to be able to transfer patterning skills to the complexities of print.

11   These words are not often easy to decipher. They are words like *said, they, the, two*, Obviously an individualized list will include these commonly used words as well, but they should be chosen carefully from words they have almost written correctly. Ignore the others for the time being.

12   What's challenging for one student may not be challenging to another. There is a growing body of research that tells us that the element of choice can motivate the brain to work better.

13   Spelling lists are readily available for schools to use as basic lists that some use to document progress year by year. However teaching aimed at students passing tests has little relevance. Rather a teacher should identify which words all learners in a classroom need in order to express themselves within the unique context of the classroom programme, their culture, and their level of creativity in language. High interest words introduced as part of new learning should be available for students to use when needed (e.g. on a blackboard or chart)

14   The NZ Council for Educational Research is producing very good examplar kits to guide teachers in using writing samples for assessment.

15   Goal books are a very useful reference for parent interviews, which most students can lead confidently. Their goal books indicate their focus, their work demonstrates what they have done related to it, and they will have much to speak about.

16   *see "Accelerated Alphabet Learning" by H.L. Ellis.* This is an integrated curriculum programme for the first two years at school which covers many curriculum areas such as maths, music and movement, language, reading, writing skills, physical education structured around the alphabet. For information, email moonlight.bay@slingshot.co.nz

17   Sites worth exploring at this stage: mayerjohnson.com: this includes 'Boardmaker' which: adapts curriculum materials for students who need symbols and PCS APPS for iPads (to help children learn vocab, articulation, listening skills etc.)

[18] Sylvia Ashton Warner, one of New Zealand's most celebrated and influential educators of the twentieth century, called high interest words 'organic vocabulary' and constructed personal reading books around them. She was very successful in teaching non-standard English speaking children to read. She also believed she had an entry point into the child's background psyche and that this could indicate trends in the future. See *"Teacher" (published 1963)*

[19] English has a very rich vocabulary and is the only language that has, or needs, a book of synonyms or a thesaurus